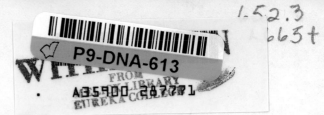
# TYPING
# MADE SIMPLE

BY

## NATHAN LEVINE, B.S. in Ed.

Instructor, Public Evening High Schools
New York City

MADE SIMPLE BOOKS
DOUBLEDAY & COMPANY, INC.
GARDEN CITY, NEW YORK

# TABLE OF CONTENTS

### LESSON 13

### LESSON 14

### LESSON 15

### LESSON 16

### LESSON 17

### LESSON 18

## LESSON 19

## LESSON 20

## LESSON 21

## LESSON 22

## LESSON 23

## LESSON 24

## LESSON 25

## LESSON 26

## LESSON 27

## LESSON 28

## LESSON 29

## LESSON 30

## LESSON 31

## LESSON 32

## LESSON 33

## LESSON 34

## LESSON 35

## SUPPLEMENTS

# ABOUT THIS BOOK

In an age when the typewriter has become an indispensable tool in business, office, school, and home, it is essential that everyone—no matter what his purpose—learn to type proficiently. The objective of **Typing Made Simple** is to teach you not only to type well, but to type expertly. Using tested, proven, *original* methods of instruction, this book will achieve that objective for you.

By simple, systematic, easy-to-understand methods, taught in clear and concise language, you learn step by step to master the whole keyboard, including the figures and special symbols; the three most popular business letter forms: Block, Semiblock, and Indented; and the latest technique for typing tabulations—by the centering method.

You are taught, in each stage of your development, what to do, how to do it, and how much time to devote to each stage. Each step in the lesson is developed gradually, to serve the needs of the beginner. You can actually measure the steady, certain progress you make as you move toward your goal of professional expertness. Each lesson refreshes your memory of the previous lesson before you go on to the next one, so that learning is *systematic* and *cumulative*. You can watch your own day-by-day progress.

**Typing Made Simple** is entirely self-teaching—although it can be, and has been, excellently used in the classroom; it is your own teacher, your own private tutor at home. In addition to the other material—including illustrations and diagrams—the book provides word-counted copy material to show you at a glance how many words you typed in a given time. Also, it teaches you how to keep your own Personal Progress Record to measure the progress you have made.

**Typing Made Simple** is a unique book in its field—there is no other like it. If your objective is typing mastery, this is the book for you.

—THE PUBLISHER

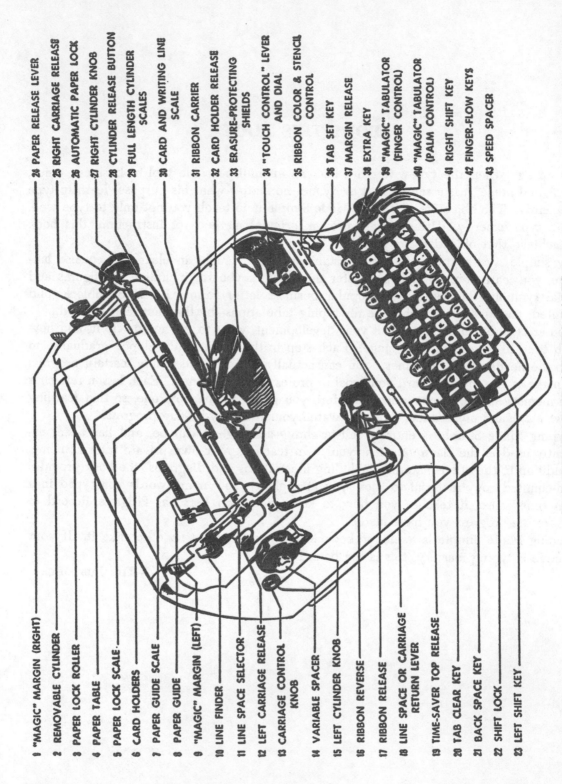

THE TYPEWRITER AND ITS PARTS
(Royal Typewriter)

24 PAPER RELEASE LEVER
25 RIGHT CARRIAGE RELEASE
26 AUTOMATIC PAPER LOCK
27 RIGHT CYLINDER KNOB
28 CYLINDER RELEASE BUTTON
29 FULL LENGTH CYLINDER SCALES
30 CARD AND WRITING LINE SCALE
31 RIBBON CARRIER
32 CARD HOLDER RELEASE
33 ERASURE-PROTECTING SHIELDS
34 "TOUCH CONTROL" LEVER AND DIAL
35 RIBBON COLOR & STENCIL CONTROL
36 TAB SET KEY
37 MARGIN RELEASE
38 EXTRA KEY
39 "MAGIC" TABULATOR (FINGER CONTROL)
40 "MAGIC" TABULATOR (PALM CONTROL)
41 RIGHT SHIFT KEY
42 FINGER-FLOW KEYS
43 SPEED SPACER

1 "MAGIC" MARGIN (RIGHT)
2 REMOVABLE CYLINDER
3 PAPER LOCK ROLLER
4 PAPER TABLE
5 PAPER LOCK SCALE
6 CARD HOLDERS
7 PAPER GUIDE SCALE
8 PAPER GUIDE
9 "MAGIC" MARGIN (LEFT)
10 LINE FINDER
11 LINE SPACE SELECTOR
12 LEFT CARRIAGE RELEASE
13 CARRIAGE CONTROL KNOB
14 VARIABLE SPACER
15 LEFT CYLINDER KNOB
16 RIBBON REVERSE
17 RIBBON RELEASE
18 LINE SPACE OR CARRIAGE RETURN LEVER
19 TIME-SAVER TOP RELEASE
20 TAB CLEAR KEY
21 BACK SPACE KEY
22 SHIFT LOCK
23 LEFT SHIFT KEY

# LESSON 1

**Aim:** To learn—
- (a) The **Home-Key** position
- (b) To use the keys **F J R U**

## Step One—Preparing To Type

**1. Center the Carriage.**

The carriage is the movable part of the typewriter that holds the cylinder.

(a) Hold the right cylinder knob and with the same hand depress the carriage release—the spring near the knob. (See Fig. 1)

(b) Move the carriage left or right and stop it at the center of the typewriter.

(c) Remove your hand from the carriage release.

Fig. 1. Centering the Carriage by Using the Carriage Release.

**2. Adjust the Paper Guide at 0.**

The paper guide is a strip of metal at the left end of the carriage; it guides the paper into the machine.

Slide the paper guide until its vertical edge points to 0 on the paper guide scale. (See Fig. 2)

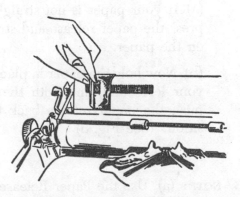

Fig. 2. Adjusting the Paper Guide at 0.

### 3. Insert the Paper.

(a) Hold the paper with the thumb and four fingers of your left hand.

(b) Place the paper squarely behind the cylinder, left edge against the paper guide.

(c) Place your thumb under the right cylinder knob and the first two fingers on top.

(d) Now give the knob a sudden spin. (See Fig. 3)

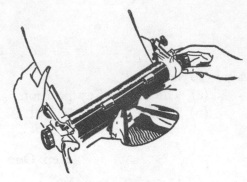

Fig. 3.  Inserting the Paper.

### 4. Adjust the Paper Bail.

Place the paper bail over the paper and move the small rollers so that they are spaced equally across the paper. (See Fig. 4)

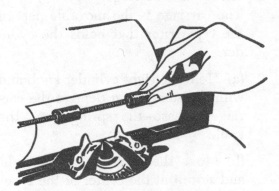

Fig. 4.  Adjusting the Paper Bail and the Small Rollers.

### 5. Straighten the Paper.

Your paper is straight if the left edge of the front part is even with the left edge of the back part—and both edges even with the paper guide.

(a) If your paper is not straight, depress the paper release and straighten the paper.

(b) Now hold the paper in place with your left hand, and with the other push the paper release back to position. (See Fig. 5)

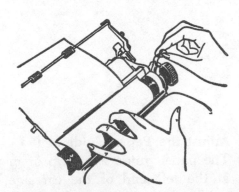

Fig. 5.  Straightening the Paper.

NOTE:  (a) Use the Paper Release to remove the paper from the machine.

(b) Return the Paper Release to position when paper is removed.

6. **Set Line Space Gauge for Single Spacing.**

The Line Space Gauge is a lever above the left end of the cylinder; it regulates the spacing between lines —single, double, or triple.

Move the Line Space Gauge to "1" for single spacing. (See Fig. 6)

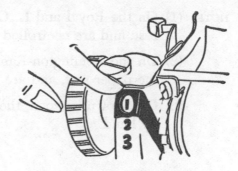

Fig. 6. Line Space Gauge at "1."

7. **Set the Margin Stops.**

The margin stops set the points at which the typing line begins and ends.

(a) Clear the margin stops now set on your machine. First move the left one to the extreme left; then move the right one to the extreme right.

(b) With a ruler, measure 5 inches on the typing line scale. This is the numbered scale indicating the length of the line that may be typed and the number of typing spaces to the inch.

(c) If 5 inches cover 50 spaces, your machine has **Pica** type—10 spaces to the inch. In this case, set your margin stops at 15 and 70.

(d) If 5 inches cover 60 spaces, your machine has **Elite** type—12 spaces to the inch. In this case, set your margin stops at 25 and 80.

Follow this procedure:

1st: Move the carriage until the printing point indicator points to the left margin; then set the margin stop.

2nd: Move the carriage until the printing point indicator points to the right margin; then set the margin stop.

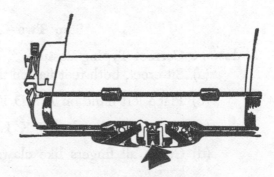

Fig. 7. Printing Point Indicator.

(See Fig. 7)

NOTE: (1) On the Royal and L. C. Smith, the margin stops are back of the paper rest, and are controlled by levers.

(2) On the Remington-Rand and R. C. Allen, the margin stops are back of the paper rest, and are controlled by hand.

(3) On the Underwood, the margin stops are at the front, and are controlled by hand.

8. **Leave a 1½ Inch Top Margin.**
You can type 6 lines to the inch from top to bottom.

(a) Turn the cylinder knob backward until the top edge of the paper is level with the alignment scale. (See Fig. 8)

(b) Strike the line-space lever 10 times with your left hand.

By typing on the 10th line from the top edge of the paper, you leave a top margin of 9 lines—1½ inches. (See Fig. 9)

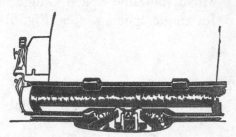

Fig. 8.  Top Edge of Paper Level with Alignment Scale.

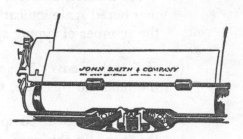

Fig. 9.  1½ Inch Top Margin (10 spaces from top edge).

## Step Two—Learning To Type

1. **Assume Correct Typing Posture.**

(a) Sit erect, both feet flat on the floor, body bent slightly forward.

(b) Place left hand on A S D F   ("Pinky" on A)

(c) Place right hand on J K L ;   ("Pinky" on ;)

(d) Curve all fingers like claws.  Rest fingertips very lightly on center of keys.

(e) Slant hands upward from the wrists.  Keep wrists low but not touching the machine.

(f) Keep elbows close to your sides.
(See Figs. 10 and 11)

**Fig. 10.** Correct Typing Posture.

## 2. How to Strike the Keys

(a) Feel the F key with the left first finger.

(b) Lift all four fingers slightly and strike the F key sharply with the fingertip.

(c) Strike the F key again—HARD. Let your finger spring back—as though the key were red hot. Strike the F key a few more times.

(d) Practice half a line of f's as shown below.

fffffffffffffffffffffffff

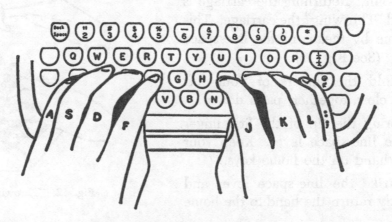

**Fig. 11.** Fingers on Home Keys.

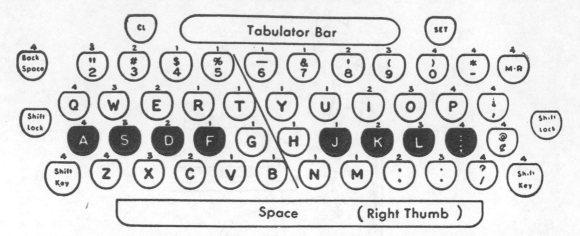

(e) Now using the right first finger, strike the J key—sharply. Release the key instantly—as though it were red hot. Try it a few more times. Practice half a line of j's. Now your line looks like this:

ffffffffffffffffffffffffjjjjjjjjjjjjjjjjjjjjjjjjjj

## 3. How to Use the Space Bar.

Spaces are made by striking the space bar, at the bottom of the keyboard, with the side of the right thumb—sharply. The left thumb does no work; so curve it slightly under the first finger.

(a) Try out the space bar by striking it quickly and sharply with the side of the right thumb.

(b) Type the following line of fff jjj, spacing between each group of letters:

fff jjj fff jjj fff jjj fff jjj fff jjj fff jjj

## 4. How to "Throw" the Carriage.

After each typewritten line, the carriage must be returned to the starting point. Returning the carriage is called "Throwing" the carriage. This is done by means of the line-space lever. (See Fig. 12)

(a) Hold the fingers of your left hand close together, palm down.

(b) Bring the tip of the first finger to the line-space lever. Keep your right hand on the home keys.

(c) Strike the line-space lever and quickly return the hand to the home keys.

Fig. 12. "Throwing" the Carriage.

5. **Self-Testing Work:** Now test yourself! See how well you can strike the F and J keys and the space bar. See how quickly you can "Throw" the carriage and return your left hand to home position. Type the following three lines exactly as shown:

TYPING TIP: *Throw the carriage with a flip of the wrist.*

```
fff jjj fff jjj fff jjj fff jjj fff jjj fff jjj
fff jjj fff jjj fff jjj fff jjj fff jjj fff jjj
fff jjj fff jjj fff jjj fff jjj fff jjj fff jjj
```

Now stop typing and **relax.**

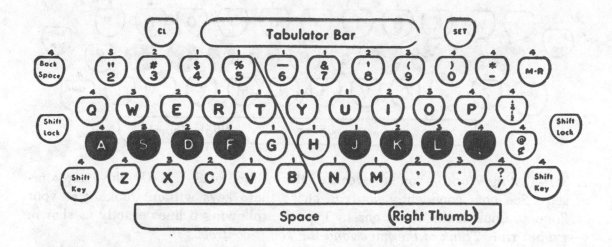

6. **Learning to use New Keys: R U**

    R is controlled by the F finger.
    U is controlled by the J finger.

### Step 1—New Key Preview
#### (Feeling the Keys—to Memorize the Reach)

**R:** Look at the keyboard. To reach R, move the F finger up and slightly to the left. Feel the center of the R key—with the fingertip. Return the finger quickly to the F key. Reach for R and return to F—several times. Try it without looking at the keyboard. Look at the above chart.

**U:** To reach U, move the J finger up and slightly to the left. Feel the center of the U key—with the fingertip. Return the finger quickly to the J key. Reach for U and return to J—several times. Try it without looking at the keyboard. Look at the above chart.

### Step 2—New Key Tryout

*Strike Keys Sharply.*

```
r r r r frf frf frf frf u u u u juj juj juj juj
frf juj frf juj frf juj frf juj frf juj frf juj
```

Now stop typing and **relax**.

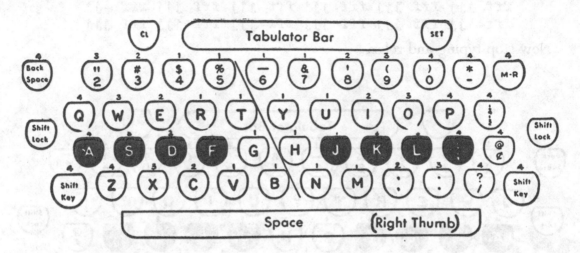

7. **Self-Testing Work:**   You have learned the location of **F J R U.** Now test your-self.   See how confidently you can strike these keys without looking at your fingers.   Look at the above chart.   Type the following 6 lines exactly as shown:

TYPING TIP: *Think of the finger and the key it controls.*

*Throw the carriage twice after every second line.*

```
fff jjj fff jjj fff jjj fff jjj fff jjj fff jjj
fff jjj fff jjj fff jjj fff jjj fff jjj fff jjj

fru fru fru jur jur jur ruj ruj ruj urf urf urf
fur fur fur ruf ruf ruf urj urj urj fuj fuj fuj

urf urf urf juf juf juf fuj fuj fuj fru fru fru
fur fur fur ruf ruf ruf urf urf urf jur jur jur
```

Now take a moment to relax.

8. **Improvement Work:**  Type another copy of the above 6 lines.  See if you can type them more smoothly and more accurately.

# LESSON 2

**Aim:** To learn to use **D K E I**

### 1. Machine Adjustments:

(a) Paper Guide: At 0.

(b) Line-Space Gauge: For single spacing.

(c) Margin Stops: For **Pica** type.........................at 15 and 70.

For **Elite** type.........................at 25 and 80.

(d) Top Margin: 1½ inches. (Type on 10th line from top edge.)

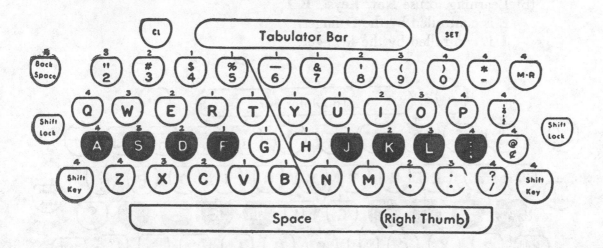

### 2. Warmup:

(5 Minutes) Type the following four lines exactly as shown. If you finish ahead of time, type them again.

REMINDER: Strike the space bar with the side of your right thumb.

*Throw the carriage twice after the second line.*

```
fff jjj fff jjj fff jjj fff jjj fff jjj fff jjj
frf juj frf juj frf juj frf juj frf juj frf juj

fur fur fur ruf ruf ruf jur jur jur ruj ruj ruj
urj urj urj juf juf juf fuj fuj fuj fur fur fur
```

### 3. New Key Control: (10 Minutes)

(a) Learning to use New Keys: **D K**

**D** is controlled by the second finger of your left hand.

**K** is controlled by the second finger of your right hand.

19

### Step 1—New Key Preview
### (Feeling the Keys—to Memorize the Reach)

Feel the center of the **D** and **K** keys. As you feel each key, think of the finger and the key it controls.

To type **D** and **K**, raise all four fingers slightly from the wrist and strike the key sharply with the fingertip. Strike the key as though it were red hot. Keep all fingers curved like claws—close to home keys.

### Step 2—New Key Tryout

d d d d ddd ddd ddd ddd k k k k kkk kkk kkk kkk
ddd kkk ddd kkk ddd kkk ddd kkk ddd kkk ddd kkk

(b) Learning to use **New Keys: E I**
     **E** is controlled by the **D** finger.
     **I** is controlled by the **K** finger.

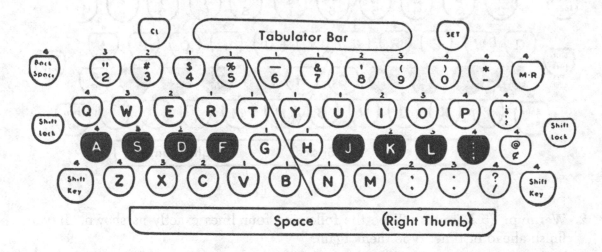

### Step 1—New Key Preview
### (Feeling the Keys—to Memorize the Reach)

**E:** To reach **E**, move the **D** finger up and slightly to the left. Feel the center of the **E** key—with the fingertip. Return the finger quickly to the **D** key. Reach for **E** and return to **D**—several times. Try it without looking at the keyboard. Look at the above chart.

**I:** To reach **I**, move the **K** finger up and slightly to the left. Feel the center of the **I** key—with the fingertip. Return the finger quickly to the **K** key. Reach for **I** and return to **K**—several times. Try it without looking at the keyboard. Look at the above chart.

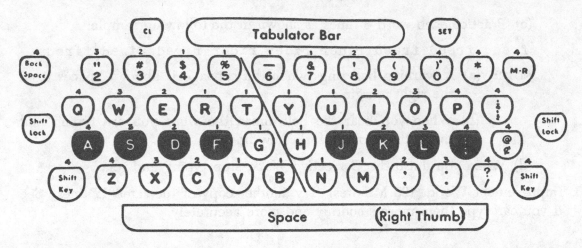

**Step 2—New Key Tryout**

```
e e e e ded ded ded ded ded i i i i kik kik kik
ded kik ded kik ded kik ded kik ded kik ded kik
```

4. **Self-Testing Work:** (25 Minutes) Test your mastery of the new keys in this lesson. Type the following 12 lines exactly as shown. Don't rush. Think of the finger and the key it controls.

TYPING TIP: *Throw the carriage with a flip of the wrist.*
*Keep right hand on home keys.*

```
did did did ire ire ire rid rid rid eke eke eke
rid rid rid eke eke eke ire ire ire did did did

kid kid kid fee fee fee red red red fir fir fir
red red red fir fir fir fee fee fee kid kid kid

free free free juke juke juke fire fire fire juke
fire fire fire juke juke juke free free free juke

deer deer deer rude rude rude dire dire dire ride
rude rude rude dire dire dire deer deer deer ride

fired fired fired rider rider rider freed freed
rider rider rider freed freed freed fired fired

did red ire fee rid deer rude fire feed juke rider
rid fee ire red did juke fire rude juke deed freed
```

5. **Corrective Work:** (10 Minutes)

(a) Compare your work carefully with the above 12 lines.

(b) Draw a line under each word in which you find an error. Write a list of these words on a separate sheet of paper.

(c) Practice each word 3 times as shown in the following sample:

```
freed freed freed rider rider rider fired fired fired
```

NOTE:  (a) A warning bell rings when the carriage is about 7 spaces from the right margin.

       (b) When you hear the bell, finish the word you are typing and throw the carriage for a new line.

(d) When you finish the **Corrective Work,** stop typing and **relax.**

6. **Improvement Work:**  (25 Minutes) Try another copy of the same 12 lines.  See if you can type them more smoothly and more accurately.

# LESSON 3

**Aim:** To learn to use the keys **T Y G H**

1. **Machine Adjustments:**
    (a) Paper Guide: At 0.
    (b) Line Space Gauge: For Single Spacing
    (c) Margin Stops: For **Pica** type.........................at 15 and 70.
                        For **Elite** type.......................at 25 and 80.
    (d) Top Margin: 1½ inches. (Type on 10th line from top edge.)

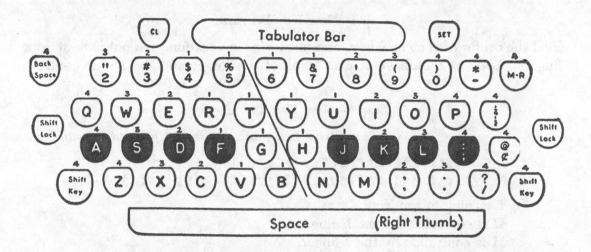

2. **Warmup:** (5 Minutes) Copy the following 6 lines exactly as shown. If you finish ahead of time, type another copy.

    TYPING TIP: *Strike keys sharply. Return fingers quickly to home keys.*

```
fff jjj ddd kkk frf juj ded kik fff jjj ddd kkk
frf juj ded kik fur fur kid kid red red ire ire

kid kid kid juke juke juke dire dire dire fire
rid rid rid rude rude rude ride ride ride feed

did red ire fee rid deer rude fire feed juke rider
rid fee ire red did juke fire rude juke deed freed
```

3. **New Key Control:** (10 Minutes)
    (a) Learning to use New Keys: **T Y**
        **T** is controlled by the **F** finger.
        **Y** is controlled by the **J** finger.

23

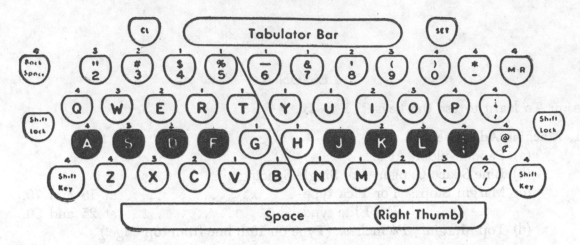

### Step 1—New Key Preview

Feel the center of each new key—and memorize its location. Do not look at your fingers. Look at the above chart. Think of the finger and the key it controls.

### Step 2—New Key Tryout

*Strike key sharply. Return finger to home base.*

```
t t t t ftf ftf ftf ftf y y y y jyj jyj jyj jyj
ftf jyj ftf jyj ftf jyj ftf jyj ftf jyj ftf jyj
```

(b) Learning to use New Keys: **G H**
     G is controlled by the F finger.
     H is controlled by the J finger.

### Step 1—New Key Preview

Reach and feel each new key several times. Return the finger quickly to home base. Memorize the new-key location. Think of the finger and the key it controls. Use the above chart as a guide.

### Step 2—New Key Tryout

*Strike sharply. Return quickly.*

```
g g g g fgf fgf fgf fgf h h h h jhj jhj jhj jhj
fgf jhj fgf jhj fgf jhj fgf jhj fgf jhj fgf jhj
```

(c) Word Drill. Containing New Keys: **T Y G H**

```
hit hit hit hit hit hit get get get get get get
yet yet yet yet yet yet try try try try try try
```

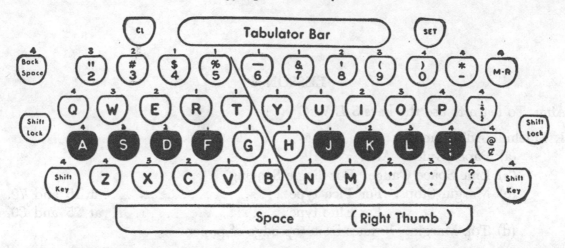

4. **Self-Testing Work:** (25 Minutes) Test your mastery of the new keys in this lesson. Copy the following 14 lines exactly as shown:

*Throw carriage twice after every second line.*

```
the the the try try try get get get yet yet yet
try try try the the the yet yet yet get get get

key key key hit hit hit tie tie tie kit kit kit
tie tie tie kit kit kit key key key hit hit hit

here here here they they they true true true
they they they true true true here here here

there there there fruit fruit fruit right right right
fruit fruit fruit right right right there there there

third third third tired tired tired urged urged urged
tired tired tired urged urged urged third third third

truth truth truth their their their dried dried dried
their their their dried dried dried truth truth truth

did they get the right dried fruit there yet
did they get the right dried fruit there yet
```

5. **Corrective Work:** (10 Minutes) Make a list of the words in which you find errors; then practice each word 3 times. REMINDER: When you hear the bell, finish the word you are typing and throw carriage for next line.

6. **Improvement Work:** (25 Minutes) Type another copy of the above 14 lines. Try to turn out a better job.

# LESSON 4

**Aim:** To learn to use the keys **S L W O**

**1. Machine Adjustments:**
    (a) Paper Guide: At 0.
    (b) Line Space Gauge: For Single Spacing.
    (c) Margin Stops: For **Pica** type.......................at 15 and 70.
                 For **Elite** type.........................at 25 and 80.
    (d) Top Margin: 10 lines from top edge of paper.

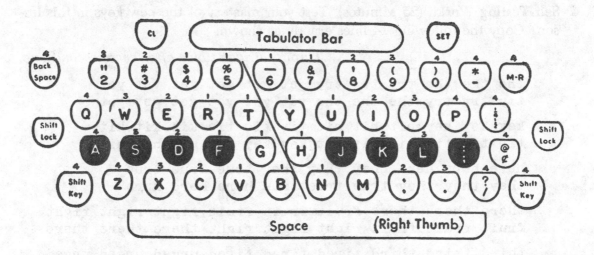

**2. Warmup:** (5 Minutes) Copy the first two lines exactly as shown; then throw the carriage twice and type the sentence 10 times.

```
frf juj ded kik ftf jyj fgf jhj frf juj ded kik
ded kik ftf jyj fgf jhj frf juj ded kik ftf jyj
```

```
they urged her to get the right dried fruit there
```

**3. New Key Control:** (10 Minutes)
    (a) Learning to use New Keys: **S L**
        **S** is controlled by the left third finger.
        **L** is controlled by the right third finger.

### Step 1—New Key Preview

Feel the center of each new key—with the fingertip. Think of the finger and the key it controls. Refer to the above chart.

26

### Step 2—New Key Tryout

*Strike keys sharply.  Let go instantly.  Keep all fingers curved.*

```
s s s s sss sss sss sss l l l l 111 111 111 111
sss 111 sss 111 sss 111 sss 111 sss 111 sss 111
```

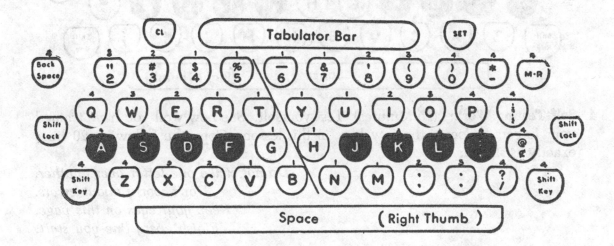

(b) Learning to use New Keys: **W O**
   **W** is controlled by the **S** finger.
   **O** is controlled by the **L** finger.

### Step 1—New Key Preview

Reach and feel each new key several times.  Return finger quickly to home base.
Memorize new-key location.  Think of the finger and the key it controls.

### Step 2—New Key Tryout

*Strike keys sharply.  Return fingers quickly to home base.*

```
w w w w sws sws sws sws o o o o lol lol lol lol
sws lol sws lol sws lol sws lol sws lol sws lol
```

(c) Word Drill.  Containing New Keys: **S L W O**

*Don't move your arms.  Let your fingers do the work.*

```
sow sow sow sow sow sow low low low low low low
row row row row row row how how how how how how
```

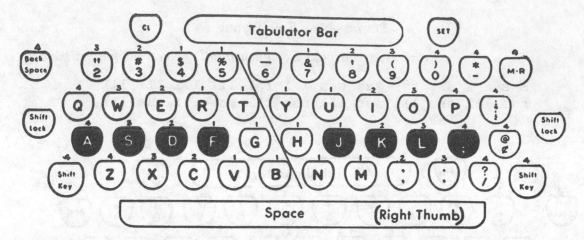

**4. Self-Testing Work:** (25 Minutes) Test yourself. See how well you have trained your fingers to locate the new keys in this lesson. Copy the following 20 lines exactly as shown:

*Do not strike one letter over another.*
*Don't worry about errors.*
*Keep your eyes on this page.*
*Finish every line you start.*

```
is is is so so so of of of do do do go go go to to to
go go go to to to do do do of of of so so so is is is

too too too low low low set set set wit wit wit wit
sit sit sit lit lit lit wit wit wit low low low low

wool wool wool suit suit suit full full full wood wood
hole hole hole wool wool wool suit suit suit good good

style style style order order order those those
loose loose loose style style style order order

desire desire desire rulers rulers rulers worker
worker worker worker desire desire desire rulers

hold your wrists low while you strike the keys
hold your wrists low while you strike the keys

we desire the right goods for our wool suits
we desire the right goods for our wool suits

if you will go with us you will see the fleet
if you will go with us you will see the fleet

we will try to fill your order for the wool suits
we will try to fill your order for the wool suits

if we get the right goods we will fill your order
if we get the right goods we will fill your order
```

5. **Corrective Work:** (10 Minutes) Check your work carefully. Make a list of the words in which you find errors; then practice each word 3 times.

6. **Improvement Work:** (25 Minutes) Type another copy of the above 20 lines. See if you can type them more smoothly and more accurately.

# LESSON 5

**Aim:** To learn to use the keys **A** ; (Semicolon) **Q P**

1. **Machine Adjustments:**
   (a) Paper Guide:  At 0.
   (b) Line Space Gauge:  For Single Spacing.
   (c) Margin Stops:  For **Pica** type . . . . . . . . . . . . . . . . . . . . . . . . . . at 15 and 70.
                    For **Elite** type . . . . . . . . . . . . . . . . . . . . . . . . at 25 and 80.
   (d) Top Margin:  10 lines from top edge of paper.

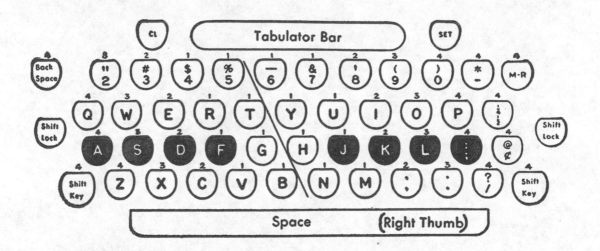

2. **Warmup:** (5 Minutes)  Copy the first two lines exactly as shown; then throw the carriage twice and type the sentence 10 times.

   ```
   frf juj ded kik ftf jyj fgf jhj frf juj ftf jyj fgf jhj
   ded kik sws lol ded kik sws lol frf juj ftf jyj fgf jhj

   we will fill your order for the wool suits this week
   ```

3. **New Key Control:**  (10 Minutes)
   (a) Learning to use New Keys: A ;
        A is controlled by the left little finger.
        ; is controlled by the right little finger.

### Step 1—New Key Preview

Feel the center of each new key—with the fingertip.  Think of the finger and the key it controls—to memorize the new-key location.

30

### Step 2—New Key Tryout

*Strike keys sharply. Keep elbows close to your sides.*

```
a a a a aaa aaa aaa aaa ; ; ; ; ;;; ;;; ;;; ;;;
aaa ;;; aaa ;;; aaa ;;; aaa ;;; aaa ;;; aaa ;;;
```

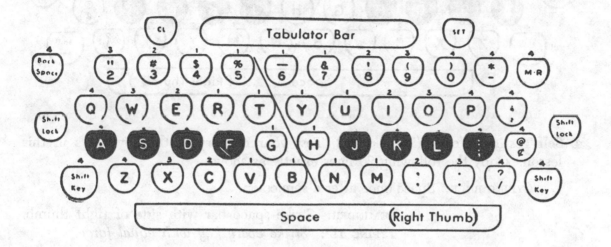

(b) Learning to use New Keys: **Q P**
    **Q** is controlled by the **A** finger.
    **P** is controlled by the **;** finger.

### Step 1—New Key Preview

Reach and feel each new key—several times. Return finger quickly to home base. Think of the finger and the key it controls—to memorize the reach.

### Step 2—New Key Tryout

*Strike keys hard.*

```
q q q q aqa aqa aqa aqa p p p p ;p; ;p; ;p; ;p;
aqa ;p; aqa ;p; aqa ;p; aqa ;p; aqa ;p; aqa ;p;
```

(c) Word Drill. Containing New Keys: **A ; Q P**

```
pa; pa; pa; pa; pa; pa; up; up; up; up; up; up;
pa; pa; pa; pa; pa; pa; up; up; up; up; up; up;

quay quay quay quay quay quip quip quip quip quip
quay quay quay quay quay quip quip quip quip quip
```

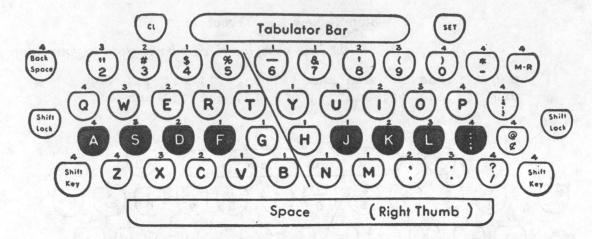

4. **Self-Testing Work:** (25 Minutes) Test your mastery of the new keys in this lesson. Copy the following 20 lines exactly as shown:

TYPING RULE: Space once after a semicolon.

REMINDER: Strike space bar with side of right thumb.
TYPING TIP: *Strike every key with equal force.*

```
apt apt apt; put put put; sip sip sip; hip hip hip;
sip sip sip; hip hip hip; apt apt apt; put put put;

quip quip quip; quit quit quit; aqua aqua aqua;
aqua aqua aqua; quip quip quip; quit quit quit;

paid paid paid; pair pair pair; pass pass pass;
pair pair pair; pass pass pass; paid paid paid;

quote quote quote; paper paper paper; quite quite;
paper paper paper; quite quite quite; quote quote;

prefer prefer prefer; prepay prepay prepay; quires;
prepay prepay prepay; prefer prefer prefer; quires;

postage postage postage; quarter quarter quarter;
poultry poultry poultry; quality quality quality;

two quires of high quality paper were shipped today;
two quires of high quality paper were shipped today;

we shall pay you well to prepare the reports for us;
we shall pay you well to prepare the reports for us;

we quote a low figure for our high quality paper;
we quote a low figure for our high quality paper;

we prefer to prepay the postage for the two quires;
we prefer to prepay the postage for the two quires;
```

5. **Corrective Work:** (10 Minutes) Check your work carefully. Make a list of the words in which you find errors. Practice each word 3 times.

6. **Improvement Work:** (25 Minutes) Try another copy of the above 20 lines—for better result. See if you can turn out a more accurate job.

## LESSON 6

**Aim:** To learn to use the **Shift Keys** for **Capital Letters.**

**1. Machine Adjustments:**
    (a) Paper Guide:  At 0.
    (b) Line Space Gauge:  For Single Spacing.
    (c) Margin Stops:  For **Pica** type.....................at 15 and 70.
                     For **Elite** type.....................at 25 and 80.
    (d) Top Margin:  10 lines from top edge of paper.

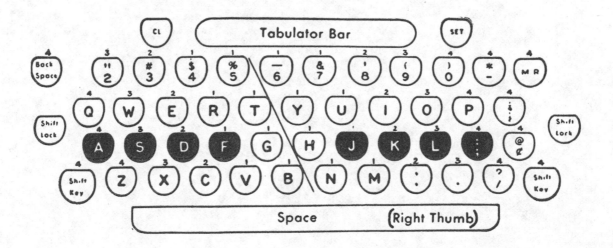

**2. Warmup:** (5 Minutes)  Copy the first two lines exactly as shown; then throw the carriage twice and type the sentence 10 times.  The sentence contains every letter you have learned thus far.

```
frf juj ftf jyj fgf jhj ded kik sws lol aqa ;p;
aqa ;p; sws lol ded kik frf juj ftf jyj fgf jhj

he will pay jed squire for the sugar this week;
```

**3. New Key Control:** (10 Minutes)  Learning to use the **shift keys.**
        To make a **Capital letter,** depress the **shift key** firmly with the little finger of the opposite hand and strike the letter to be **capitalized.**  Be sure to hold the **shift key** down until you have struck the letter.

34

## Step 1—Shift Key Tryout

(a) Depress the left **shift key**; then return the finger to **A**.
(b) Depress the right **shift key**; then return the finger to semicolon.
(c) Practice the left and right **shift key** manipulation until you can perform it smoothly. (See Figs. 13, 14)

Fig. 13. Using Left Shift Key.

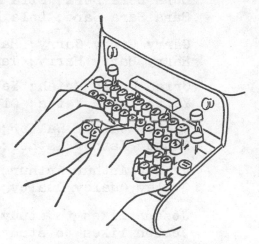

Fig. 14. Using Right Shift Key.

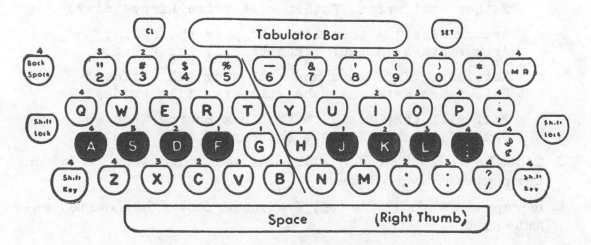

## Step 2—Capital Letter Drill

*Hold down the shift key until you have struck the letter.*
*Return the little finger quickly to its home key.*

F F F F F F F Fa Fa Fa Fa Fa Fa Fay Fay Fay Fay Fay Fay
J J J J J J J Ja Ja Ja Ja Ja Ja Jay Jay Jay Jay Jay Jay

R R R R R R R Ra Ra Ra Ra Ra Ra Ray Ray Ray Ray Ray Ray
H H H H H H H Ha Ha Ha Ha Ha Ha Hal Hal Hal Hal Hal Hal

4. **Self-Testing Work:** (25 Minutes) Test your mastery of the **shift key.** Copy the following 20 lines exactly as shown:

REMINDER: Space once after a semicolon.

```
Kay Kay Kay; Joe Joe Joe; Alf Alf Alf; Lou Lou Lou;
Joe Joe Joe; Kay Kay Kay; Lou Lou Lou; Alf Alf Alf;

Dora Dora Dora; Ella Ella Ella; Pete Pete Pete;
Sara Sara Sara; Lola Lola Lola; Will Will Will;

Garry Garry Garry; Harry Harry Harry; Paula Paula;
Harry Harry Harry; Taffy Taffy Taffy; Quill Quill;

Uriah Uriah Uriah; Yetta Yetta Yetta; Ollie Ollie;
Yetta Yetta Yetta; Ollie Ollie Ollie; Uriah Uriah;

Walter Walter Walter; Esther Esther Esther; Isaiah;
Esther Esther Esther; Walter Walter Walter; Isaiah;

Arthur Arthur Arthur; Lester Lester Lester; Philip;
Qualey Qualey Qualey; Arthur Arthur Arthur; Philip;

Joseph likes to study; Joseph likes to study art;
Joseph likes to study; Joseph likes to study art;

Esther will write; Esther will write Larry today;
Esther will write; Esther will write Larry today;

Arthur likes; Arthur likes to play the flute;
Arthur likes; Arthur likes to play the flute;

Kate says; Kate says she will stay till Friday;
Kate says; Kate says she will stay till Friday;

Paul will take Willa to the Park Sherry Theater;
Paul will take Willa to the Park Sherry Theater;
```

5. **Corrective Work:** (10 Minutes) Make a list of the words in which you find errors; then practice each word 3 times.

6. **Improvement Work:** (25 Minutes) Type another copy of the above 20 lines—for better result.

# LESSON 7

**Aim:** (a) To learn to use the **Shift Lock.**

(b) To learn to use the **:** (Colon).

## 1. Machine Adjustments:

(a) Paper Guide: At 0.

(b) Line Space Gauge: For Single Spacing.

(c) Margin Stops: For **Pica** type . . . . . . . . . . . . . . . . . . . . . . . . . . . . . . at 15 and 70.

For **Elite** type . . . . . . . . . . . . . . . . . . . . . . . . . . at 25 and 80.

(d) Top Margin: 10 lines from top edge of paper.

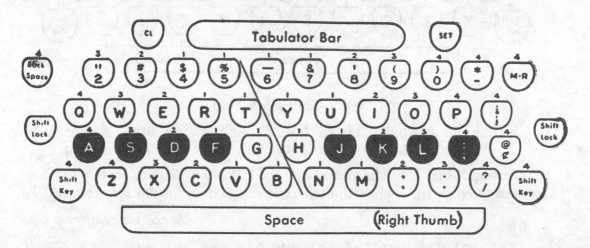

## 2. Warmup:

(5 Minutes) Copy the first two lines exactly as shown; then throw the carriage twice and type the sentence 10 times—to give you a good workout on all the letters you have learned so far.

```
frf juj ftf jyj fgf jhj ded kik sws lol aqa ;p;
aqa ;p; sws lol ded kik frf juj ftf jyj fgf jhj
```

```
He will pay Jed Squire for the sugar this week;
```

## 3. New Key Control:

(10 Minutes) Learning to use the shift lock. The shift lock is a time-saving device which enables you to type a series of **capital letters.**

### Step 1—Shift Lock Tryout

(a) With your left little finger, depress the shift lock—then return the finger quickly to its home key. The machine is now **locked** for typing **capital letters.**

37

(b) Now with the same little finger, strike the **shift key**—then return the finger quickly to its home key.  The machine is now unlocked—for regular typing.

(c) Repeat the above exercise several times until you develop the knack of **locking** and unlocking the machine.

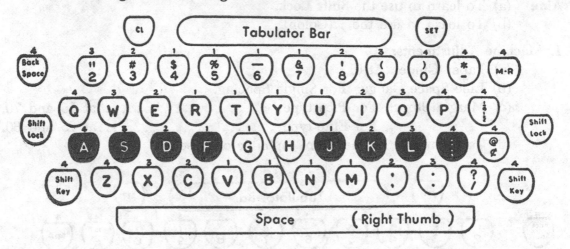

**Step 2—Shift Lock Drill**

```
It is GOOD WORK; It is GOOD WORK; It is GOOD WORK;
It is GOOD WORK; It is GOOD WORK; It is GOOD WORK;
```

4. **Self-Testing Work:**  (20 Minutes) Copy the following 15 lines exactly as shown. To make a colon (:), depress the left shift key and strike the semicolon (;) key.

*Space twice after a colon.*

```
frf juj ftf jyj fgf jhj ded kik sws lol aqa ;p;
The TITLE of the REPORT is:   HOUSES FOR SALE
The TITLE of the REPORT is:   HOUSES FOR SALE

aqa ;p; sws lol ded kik frf juj ftf jyj fgf jhj
We quote LOW FIGURES for HIGHEST QUALITY paper;
We quote LOW FIGURES for HIGHEST QUALITY paper;

frf juj ftf jyj fgf jhj ded kik sws lol aqa ;p;
The PARK POSTER reads:   KEEP OFF THE GRASS
The PARK POSTER reads:   KEEP OFF THE GRASS

aqa ;p; sws lol ded kik frf juj ftf jyj fgf jhj
Paul quoted the old adage:   THE THRIFTY ARE WISE
Paul quoted the old adage:   THE THRIFTY ARE WISE

frf juj ftf jyj fgf jhj ded kik sws lol aqa ;p;
You should STRIKE ALL THE KEYS with EQUAL POWER;
You should STRIKE ALL THE KEYS with EQUAL POWER;
```

**5. Corrective Work:** (10 Minutes) Make a list of the words in which you find errors; then practice each word 3 times.

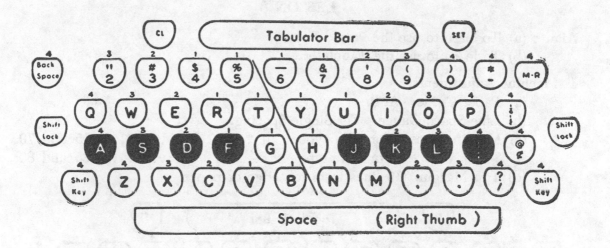

**6. Improvement Work:** (20 Minutes) Type another copy of the 15 lines (p. 38)—to strengthen your control of the **shift lock** and the **shift key.**

**7. Challenge Work:** (10 Minutes) Here's a challenge to you: 9 new lines. Try for a **perfect** copy.

*Keep your mind on your work. Think as you type.*

```
frf juj ftf jyj fgf jhj ded kik sws lol aqa ;p;
GOOD WORK will lead to a HAPPY LIFE for you;
GOOD WORK will lead to a HAPPY LIFE for you;

aqa ;p; sws lol ded kik frf juj ftf jyj fgf jhj
The DAILY DRILLS will HELP YOU type with EASE;
The DAILY DRILLS will HELP YOU type with EASE;

frf juj ftf jyj fgf jhj ded kik sws lol aqa ;p;
GOOD SALARIES are USUALLY PAID to FAST TYPISTS;
GOOD SALARIES are USUALLY PAID to FAST TYPISTS;
```

# LESSON 8

**Aim:**  (a) To learn to use the **Period Key**.
         (b) To learn to use the **Tabulator**.

## 1. Machine Adjustments:
   (a) Paper Guide:  At 0.
   (b) Line Space Gauge:  For Single Spacing.
   (c) Margin Stops:  For **Pica** type . . . . . . . . . . . . . . . . . . . . . . . . . . . . . . at 15 and 70.
                     For **Elite** type . . . . . . . . . . . . . . . . . . . . . . . at 25 and 80.
   (d) Top Margin:  10 lines from top edge of paper.

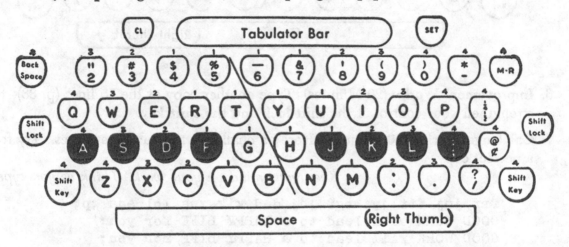

## 2. Warmup: (5 Minutes) Copy the first two lines exactly as shown; then throw the carriage twice and type the sentence 10 times—to strengthen your control of all the keys you have learned so far.

```
frf juj ftf jyj fgf jhj ded kik sws lol aqa ;p;
aqa ;p; sws lol ded kik frf juj ftf jyj fgf jhj

He will pay Jed Squire for the sugar this week;
```

## 3. New Key Control:  (10 Minutes)
   (a) Learning to use the **Period Key**.
       The **L** finger controls the **period key**.

### Step 1—New Key Preview

Feel the center of the **period key**—with the fingertip; then return the finger to the **L** key.  Repeat this procedure several times—thinking of the **L** finger and the **period key** which it controls.

40

### Step 2—New Key Tryout

*Space twice after period at end of a sentence.*

```
. . . . . . l.l l.l l.l l.l l.l l.l l.l l.l l.l
Hit it lightly.  Hit it lightly.  Hit it lightly.
Hit it lightly.  Hit it lightly.  Hit it lightly.
```

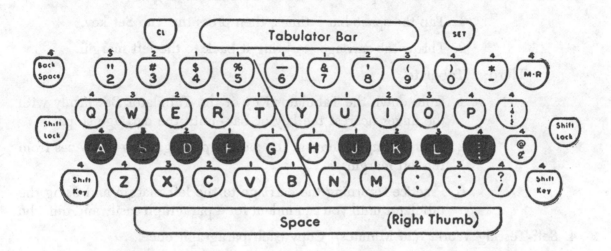

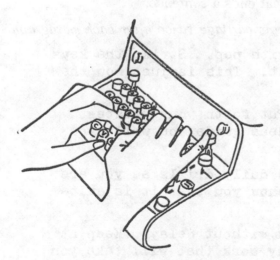

Fig. 15. Using the Tabulator Key.

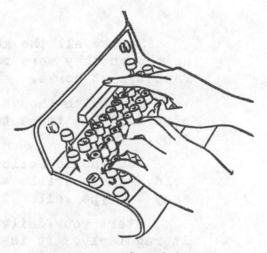

Fig. 16. Using the Tabulator Bar.

(b) Learning to use the **Tabulator**.

Your typewriter has a tabulator key or a tabulator bar with which you you can make the carriage jump to any scale points you wish. (See Figs. 15, 16)

Follow these steps for indenting paragraphs:

First:      Remove **Tab Stops** Already Set.

1. Move the carriage to the extreme left.

2. Hold down the **clear** key and throw the carriage—to bring it back to the left margin.

Second:   Set a **Tab Stop** 5 Spaces From Your Left Margin.

1. Tap the space bar 5 times; then press the **Tab Set** key.

2. Throw the carriage—to bring it back to the left margin.

Third:     Tabulate.

1. Hold down the Tabulator Key or the Tabulator Bar firmly with the finger nearest the key or bar—until the carriage stops.

2. Your carriage is now at the paragraph beginning—5 spaces from the left margin.

3. Practice returning the carriage to the left margin and using the tabulator until you can indent for a paragraph easily and quickly.

4. **Self-Testing Work:** (20 Minutes) Copy each paragraph **once**.

REMINDER:  Space **twice** after a period that ends a sentence.

*Throw carriage twice after each paragraph.*

```
    Strike all the keys with pep.  Strike the keys
as though they were red hot.  This is just how the
fast typist works.

    Type with thought.  Put forth your greatest
efforts.  Let these two ideas guide you while you
type.

    You should follow the daily drills as you are
told.  These drills will show you that it is quite
easy to type well.

    Start your daily work without delay.  Keep at
it regularly.  It is steady work that will take you
to your goal.
```

5. **Corrective Work:** (10 Minutes) Make a list of the words in which you find errors; then practice each word 3 times.

6. **Improvement Work:** (20 Minutes) Type another copy of the above 4 paragraphs. Remember: Your aim in the **improvement work** is to turn out a **better job**.

Now **relax** for a moment.

**7. Keyboard Review:** (10 Minutes) The following 8 lines will help you to strengthen your control of **F J R U.** Copy them exactly as shown. If you finish ahead of time, type them again—to see if you can turn out a **perfect job.**

*Throw carriage twice after every second line.*

```
for fat few fur foe fit fed fee for fat fir few fro;
fro few fir fat for fee fig foe fop fit fur fat fad;

jug jig jut jar joy jag jaw jar jet jot jog jug joy;
joy jug jog jag jaw joy jig jut jar jig jaw jog jet;

rye rut row red rip ray rap rug rig rut rye rug rot;
rot rye rut row red rip ray rap rug rig rut rye rug;

up us use uses urge ugly usage upper uproar upright;
us up use urge uses urge urges udder utters upstart;
```

# LESSON 9

**Aim:**   (a) To boost your typing skill by 1-minute timings.
      (b) To learn to use the keys **V M**

## 1. Machine Adjustments:

    (a) Paper Guide:  At 0.
    (b) Line Space Gauge:  For Single Spacing.
    (c) Margin Stops:  For **Pica** type.............................at 15 and 70.
                    For **Elite** type.............................at 25 and 80.
    (d) Top Margin:  10 lines from top edge of paper.

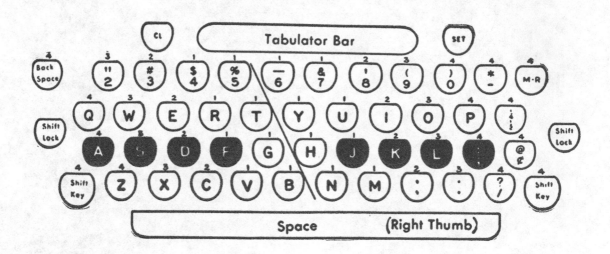

## 2. Warmup:

(5 Minutes) Copy the first two lines exactly as shown; then throw the carriage twice and type the sentence ten times.

```
frf juj ftf jyj fgf jhj ded kik sws lol aqa ;p;
aqa ;p; sws lol ded kik frf juj ftf jyj fgf jhj
```

I will pay Joe Quig for the sugar today.
     1     2     3     4     5     6     7     8

NOTE: (a) The above **warm-up** sentence contains 8 five-stroke words. A stroke means a letter, a space, or a punctuation mark.

        (b) In calculating typing speed, 5 strokes count as 1 word.

3. **Skill-Building Work:** (10 Minutes) One good way to boost your skill is to type a sentence over and over, trying hard to improve each time you repeat it.

### One-Minute Timed Test

Using a watch with a second hand, time yourself on the **warm-up** sentence, p. 44, for 1 minute. If possible, ask a friend or a member of your family to time you.

Repeat the sentence as many times as you can before the end of the minute. Then—

(a) Jot down the number of words you typed and the number of errors you made.

(b) Subtract 1 for each error from the total words you typed. The answer shows the number of correct words you typed in one minute.

> EXAMPLE: Assume that you typed 17 words and made 3 errors.
> Total Words Typed...................... 17
> Subtract: (3 errors x 1).................. –3
> Correct Words Typed............. 14

(c) Take 2 more 1-minute timings. After each timing, see how many Correct Words you typed. Jot down the number.

(d) Now compare the results of all the 1-minute timings. See in which timing you typed the most **correct words.** That is your best score.

(e) Keep a Personal Progress Record of your best scores in the form of a table like the following sample:

### 1-Minute Timed Typing
#### Score Sheet

| Lesson | Correct Words |
| --- | --- |
| 9 | 14 |

TYPING TIP: *After each timing, practice the words in which you made errors until you can type them smoothly and accurately.*

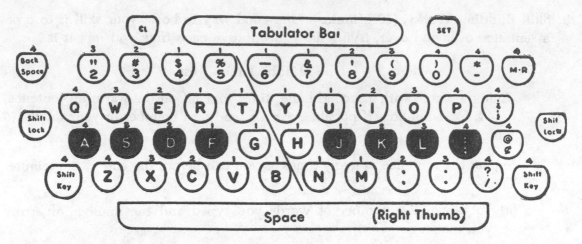

**4. New Key Control:** (10 Minutes)
   (a) Learning to use New Keys: **V M**
   **V** is controlled by the **F** finger.
   **M** is controlled by the **J** finger.

### Step 1—New Key Preview

Feel the center of each new key—with the fingertip; then return the finger to its home base. Repeat this procedure several times. Think of the finger and the key it controls—to memorize the reach for the new keys.

### Step 2—New Key Tryout

```
v v v v fvf fvf fvf fvf m m m m jmj jmj jmj jmj
fvf jmj fvf jmj fvf jmj fvf jmj fvf jmj fvf jmj
```

   (b) Word Drill. Containing New Keys: **V M**

```
vim vim vim vim vim vim met met met met met met
vim vim vim vim vim vim met met met met met met
```

**5. Self-Testing Work:** (25 Minutes) Part 1. Words and sentences. Copy the following 8 lines exactly as shown.

REMINDER: Space once after a semicolon.

```
over over over; gave gave gave; have have have;
home home home; seem seem seem; time time time;

ever ever ever; more more more; item item item;
live live live; vast vast vast; five five five;

You must devote more time to your daily work.
You must devote more time to your daily work.

You should go over every item with more thought.
You should go over every item with more thought.
```

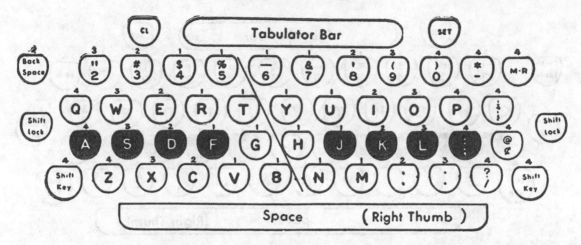

**Part 2.** Paragraph Practice. Copy each paragraph ONCE.

    1st: Remove all stops

    2nd: Set a tab stop:   For **Pica** type. . . . . ⊡. . . . . . . . ⊡. . .⊡. . . . . . . .at 20.
                    For **Elite** type. . . . . . . . . . . .⊡. . . . . . .⊡. . .at 30.

    3rd: Set line space gauge for **double** spacing

                  *Double spacing has one blank line between typed lines.*

           REMINDER: Space twice after a period that ends a sentence.

```
        You will surely make good if you give more time

to your daily work here.  You must make every effort

to make good.

        You will improve your skill every day if you

devote some thought to your work.  You will surely

progress if you keep at your work regularly.  Just

have faith.

        Skillful typists make very good salaries.  All

types of firms require them.  So try your utmost to

develop your skill.
```

**6. Corrective Work:**  (10 Minutes) Make a list of the words in which you find errors; then practice each word 3 times.

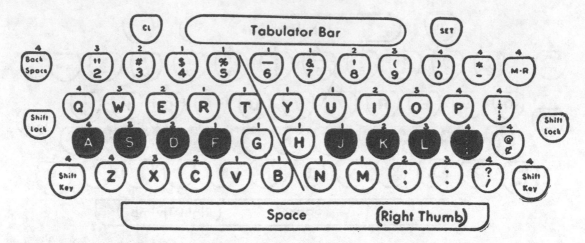

7. **Improvement Work:** (10 Minutes) Type another copy of the same 3 paragraphs. Try for smoother and more accurate typing.

8. **Challenge Work:** (5 Minutes) Another challenge to you! Here are 8 new lines containing the letters **G H T Y**....to test your mastery of them. See if you can turn out a **perfect** copy.

*Set Line Space Gauge for single spacing.*
*Throw the carriage twice after every second line.*

```
go got get gas gag gap gay gig gray greed great;
go gig gay gap gas gag get gas gray great greed;

her has had his hit hot hut hat hay hag had his;
his had hag hay hat hut hot hit his had has her;

to try tip tap two tag too to try tip tap two;
to two tap tip try too try to top tap tag try;

you yes yet yap yell year yoke your yowl yore;
yap yet yes you yore yowl your yoke year yell;
```

# LESSON 10

**Aim:** (a) To boost your typing skill by 1-minute timings.

(b) To learn to use the keys **B N**

## 1. Machine Adjustments:

(a) Paper Guide:  At 0.

(b) Line Space Gauge:  For Single Spacing.

(c) Margin Stops:  For **Pica** type.........................at 15 and 70.

For **Elite** type.........................at 25 and 80.

(d) Top Margin:  10 lines from top edge of paper.

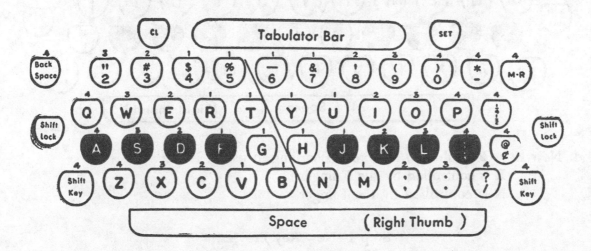

## 2. Warmup: (5 Minutes) Copy the first two lines exactly as shown; then throw the carriage twice and type the sentence ten times:

```
frf juj ftf jyj fgf jhj ded kik sws lol aqa ;p;
fgf jhj fvf jmj fgf jhj fvf jmj fgf jhj fvf jmj

Paul Quigs will devote more time to his work.
    1   2   3   4   5   6   7   8   9
```

*5 strokes count as 1 word.*

## 3. Skill-Building Work: (10 Minutes) As in Lesson 9, take three 1-minute timings on the **warm-up** sentence. Repeat it as many times as you can before the end of the minute. Then—

(a) Jot down the number of words you typed and the number of errors you made.

49

(b) Subtract 1 for each error from the total words you typed. The answer shows the most Correct Words you typed in one minute.

(c) See in which timing you typed the most Correct Words. That is your best score. Enter it in your Personal Progress Record—the 1-Minute Timed Typing Score Sheet which you established in Lesson 9.

REMINDER: After each timing, practice the words in which you made errors until you can type them smoothly and accurately.

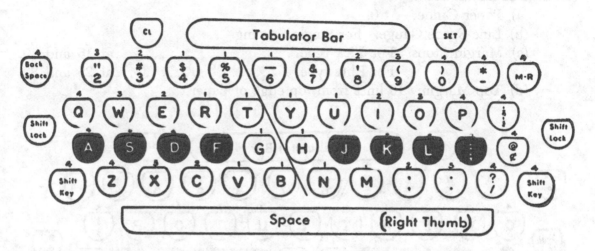

4. **New Key Control:** (10 Minutes) Learning to use **B N**
   B is controlled by the F finger.
   N is controlled by the J finger.

### Step 1—New Key Preview

Feel the center of each new key—with the fingertip; then return the finger quickly to its home base. Repeat this fingering several times. Think of the finger and the key it controls—to memorize the new key location.

### Step 2—New Key Tryout

b b b b fbf fbf fbf fbf n n n n jnj jnj jnj jnj
fbf jnj fbf jnj fbf jnj fbf jnj fbf jnj fbf jnj

### Step 3—Word Drill

bin bin bin bin bin bin nib nib nib nib nib nib
big big big big big big now now now now now now

5. **Self-Testing Work:** (25 Minutes) Part 1. Words and Sentences. Copy the following 8 lines exactly as shown:

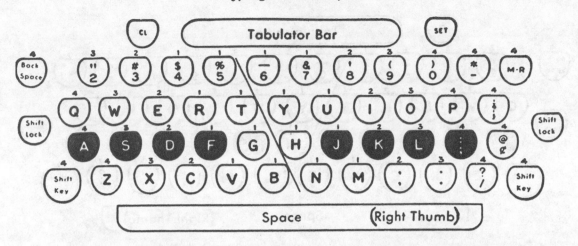

*Aim for Accuracy.*

bun bun bun; nip nip nip; fib fib fib; win win win;
fib fib fib; win win win; bun bun bun; nip nip nip;

bent bent bent; nine nine nine; vent vent vent;
mend mend mend; vine vine vine; blow blow blow;

We require more time to turn out a very good job.
We require more time to turn out a very good job.

Be prompt.   Never shirk.   Make promptness a habit.
Be prompt.   Never shirk.   Make promptness a habit.

Part 2.   Paragraph Practice.

Step 1.   Remove all stops.

Step 2.   Set Tab Stops:  For **Pica** type . . . . . . . . . . . . . . . . . . . . . . . at 20.
For **Elite** type . . . . . . . . . . . . . . . . . . . . . . at 30.

Step 3.   Set Line Space Gauge for **double** spacing.

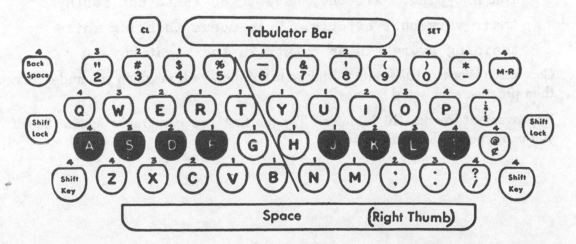

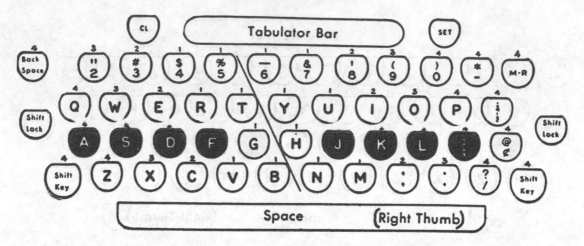

**C**opy each paragraph **once.**

*Your machine is now set for double spacing.*
*Throw carriage once after each line and after each paragraph.*

REMINDER: Space twice after a Colon.

Never put off until tomorrow any job you should finish today.  Try to be prompt at all times.  No one likes to be kept waiting.

Keep on working just as diligently as you have been doing up to this point.  You will soon be a master of the keyboard.  You will have a valuable skill that will repay you for your efforts.

Remember this:  Every boy and girl is able to learn typing.  All they have to do is to put forth their very best efforts.  This means thinking while training every finger to strike the right key.

6. **Corrective Work:**  (10 Minutes) Make a list of the words in which you find errors; then practice each word 3 times.

7. **Improvement Work:**  (10 Minutes) Try the first two paragraphs again.  See if you can type the first one **perfectly.**

8. **Challenge Work:** (5 Minutes) The following 8 lines give you a good review of the letters **D E K I.** Challenge yourself to turn out a **perfect** copy.

*Keep your eyes here. Every line is different.*

```
do dot due dye day dew dab den dim dog die dig dry dip
do dig dry dip die dog dim dab den dew day dye due dot

ebb eke err eve end egg ever even edge earn east evil
err eke eve end ebb eel evil east earn edge envy easy

kid kin kit keg key king kind know knee knot knew
key keg kid kit kin knew knot knee knob king kind

it is in if ire ill ink inn imp idle item isle iron
if in is it imp inn ill ire ink item idle iron isle
```

# LESSON 11

**Aim:** (a) To boost your typing skill by 1-minute timings.
      (b) To learn to use **C** **,** (Comma)

**1. Machine Adjustments:**
    (a) Paper Guide: At 0.
    (b) Line Space Gauge: For Single Spacing.
    (c) Margin Stops: For **Pica** type . . . . . . . . . . . . . . . . . . . . . . . . . . . . . . at 15 and 70.
                   For **Elite** type . . . . . . . . . . . . . . . . . . . . . . . . . . at 25 and 80.
    (d) Top Margin: 10 lines from top edge of paper.

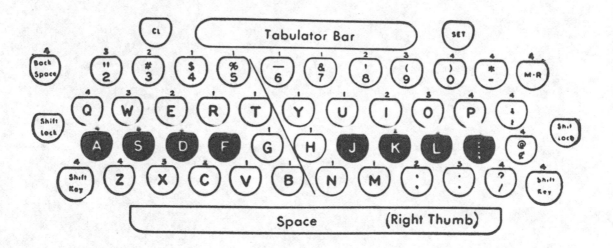

**2. Warmup:** (5 Minutes) Copy the first two lines exactly as shown; then throw the carriage twice and type the sentence 10 times.

```
frf juj ftf jyj fgf jhj ded kik sws lol aqa ;p;
fvf jmj fbf jnj fvf jmj fbf jnj fvf jmj fbf jnj
```

The Ben Mavis firm submitted the lowest quotation.
    1     2     3     4     5     6     7     8     9    10

**3. Skill-Building Work:** (10 Minutes) As before, take 3 one-minute timings on the **warm-up** sentence. Repeat it as many times as you can before the end of the minute. Then—

    (a) Jot down the number of words you typed and the number of errors you made.

(b) Subtract 1 for each error from the total words you typed. The answer shows the most Correct Words you typed in one minute.

(c) See in which timing you typed the most Correct Words. That is your best score. Enter it in your Personal Progress Record.

REMINDER: After each timing, practice the words in which you made errors until you can type them smoothly and accurately.

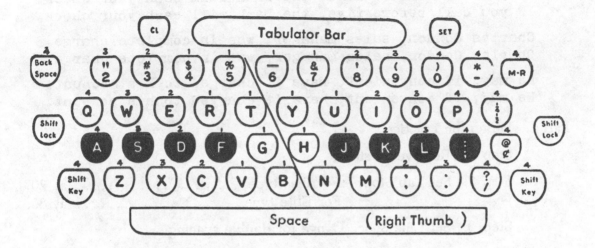

4. **New Key Control:** (10 Minutes) Learning to use New Keys: **C** ,

  **C** is controlled by the **D** finger.

  **,** is controlled by the **K** finger.

### Step 1—New Key Preview

Feel the center of each new key—with the fingertip; then return the finger quickly to its home base. Repeat this fingering several times—thinking of the finger and the key it controls.

### Step 2—New Key Tryout

*Strike comma lightly.*

c c c c dcd dcd dcd dcd , , , , k,k k,k k,k k,k
dcd k,k dcd k,k dcd k,k dcd k,k dcd k,k dcd k,k

### Step 3—Word Drill

can, can, can, can, can, cue, cue, cue, cue, cue,
can, can, can, can, can, cue, cue, cue, cue, cue,

**5. Self-Testing Work:** (30 Minutes)  Part 1.  Words and Sentences.  Copy the following 10 lines exactly as shown:

TYPING RULE: Space once after a comma.

```
cash, cash, cash, lack, lack, lack, lace, lace, lace,
lack, lack, lack, lace, lace, lace, cash, cash, cash,

could, could, could, clerk, clerk, clerk, camp, camp,
clerk, clerk, clerk, could, could, could, cane, cane,

If you call before five, the bank will cash your check.
If you call before five, the bank will cash your check.

Charles Condon, sales manager, was in complete charge.
Charles Condon, sales manager, was in complete charge.

He may, if convenient, have it charged to his account.
He may, if convenient, have it charged to his account.
```

Part 2.  Paragraph Practice.

Step 1.  Remove all stops.

Step 2.  Set Tab Stops:  For **Pica** type . . . . . . . . . . . . . . . . . . . . . . . at 20.
For **Elite** type . . . . . . . . . . . . . . . . . . . . . at 30.

Step 3.  Set Line Space Gauge for **double** spacing.

Copy each paragraph **once**.

*Keep wrists low but not touching the machine. Return to guide keys quickly.*

```
      Space once after a comma.  Space once after a
semicolon.  Space twice after a period that ends a
sentence.  Strike each key with the same force.
      The tabulator is a device which helps you to
type faster.  It enables you to skip across the page
to any point you desire.
      First, set a tab stop at the point to which you
wish the carriage to jump.  Second, move the carriage
back to the left margin.  Third, hold the tabulator
bar or the tabulator key down until the carriage has
stopped.
```

**6. Corrective Work:** (10 Minutes)  Make a list of the words in which you find errors; then practice each word 3 times.

REMINDER: When you hear the bell, finish the word you are typing and throw the carriage for the next line.

7. **Improvement Work:** (15 Minutes) Now relax a moment! Then type another copy of the above 3 paragraphs. This time, try to type them more smoothly and more accurately. Try for real improvement.

8. **Challenge Work:** (5 Minutes) The following 8 lines test your mastery of **S W L O**. Challenge yourself to a **perfect** copy.

*Keep your eyes here.*

```
sub sum see sun set sit sin sip she ship shall shame
sit sin sip set sub sum see sod sob slip sweep super

won win who why wet was weak wear west well what when
was wet why who win won what well wear west when what

lad lid lot let log lie lag lug lip last late lawn
lip lag lug lie log let lot lid lad land lane last

own out owl old one oak out oil off over oven open
off oil out oak one old owl our own open ours over
```

# LESSON 12

**Aim:** (a) To boost your typing skill by 2-minute timings.

(b) To learn to use **X** and to review the **period** key.

## 1. Machine Adjustments:
(a) Paper Guide:  At 0.

(b) Line Space Gauge:  For Single Spacing.

(c) Margin Stops:  For **Pica** type......................at 15 and 70.

For **Elite** type......................at 25 and 80.

(d) Top Margin:  10 lines from top edge of paper.

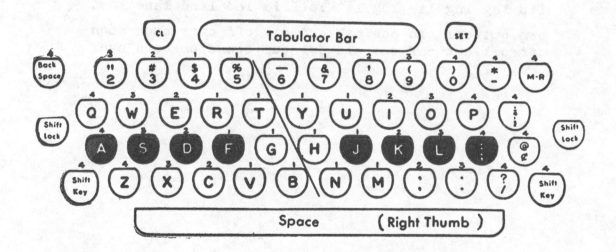

## 2. Warmup: (5 Minutes)  Copy the first two lines exactly as shown; then throw the carriage twice and type the sentence ten times.

```
frf juj ftf jyj fgf jhj fvf jmj fbf jnj fvf jmj
ded kik sws lol aqa ;p; dcd k,k dcd k,k fvf jmj
```

Mona and Bert are making plans for their vacation.

## 3. Skill-Building Work: (15 Minutes)  This consists of:
(a) Preview Practice on Words and Phrases................. 3 minutes

(b) Three 2-Minute Timings and Word Practice.............. 12 minutes

15 minutes

**First:**     **Preview Practice.** To prepare yourself for the 2-minute timings, practice each of the following words and phrases three times.

58

```
touch...learn...above...typing...talent...
average...special...that is...You do......
You do not
```

**Second: Machine Adjustments.**

    (a) Remove all tab stops.

    (b) Set a tab stop 5 spaces from your left margin.

    (c) Set line space gauge for **double** spacing.

**Third: Three 2-Minute Timings.**

    Time yourself for 2 minutes on the following paragraph. Repeat it if you finish before the end of 2 minutes.

*Figures indicate number of 5-stroke words.*

```
                        5
     Touch typing is easy to learn.  You do not need
  10                          15
a mind that is above the average.  You do not even
   20                          25   26
need a special talent for typing.
```

**Fourth: Calculate Your Typing Speed—after each timing.**

    (a) Jot down the total words typed and the total errors made.

    (b) Subtract 1 for each error from the total words typed.

    (c) Divide the remainder by 2—because you typed for 2 minutes. The result indicates your typing speed in Correct Words Per Minute.

        EXAMPLE: Assume that in the first 2-minute timing, you typed 29 words with 4 errors.

| | |
|---|---:|
| Total Words Typed | 29 |
| Subtract: (4 errors x 1) | –4 |
| Correct Words Typed | 2/25 |
| Correct Words Per Minute | 12½ |

        Your typing speed in Correct Words is 13 words per minute.

        NOTE: (a) Fractions ½ and over are counted as whole numbers.

                (b) Fractions less than ½ are dropped.

    (d) See in which timing you typed the most Correct Words. Consider that your best 2-minute score.

EXAMPLE: Assume that the 3 two-minute timings which you
have taken show the following results:

| Timing | Correct Words Typed |
|---|---|
| 1st.................... | 13 |
| 2nd..................[.] | 15 |
| 3rd.................... | 14 |

Your best score is in the second timing—because you
typed the most Correct Words.

REMINDER: After each timing, practice the words in which you
made errors until you can type them smoothly and
accurately.

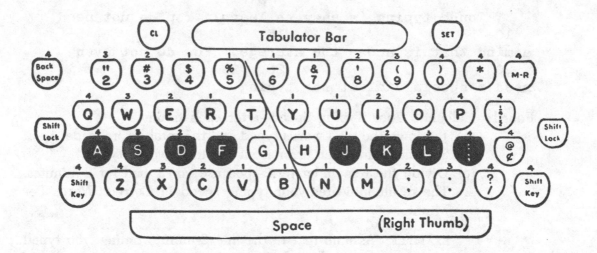

4. **New Key Control:** (10 Minutes) Learning to use **X** and **.** (Period)
   **X** is controlled by the **S** finger.
   **.** is controlled by the **L** finger.


## Step 1—New Key Preview

Feel the center of each new key—with the fingertip; then return the finger quickly
to its home base. Repeat this fingering several times—thinking of the finger and
the key it controls—to memorize the New Key location.


## Step 2—New Key Tryout

*Strike period lightly.*

```
x x x x  sxs sxs sxs sxs  . . . .  l.l l.l l.l l.l
sxs l.l sxs l.l s..s l.l sxs l.l sxs l.l sxs l.l
```

## Step 3—Word Drill

*Space once after an abbreviation.*

```
six six six six six six etc. etc. etc. etc. etc.
six six six six six six etc. etc. etc. etc. etc.
```

5. **Self-Testing Work:** (25 Minutes)

Part 1. Words and Sentences.

Copy the following 8 lines. **Single** spacing.

```
fixes fixes fixes; mixes mixes mixes; taxes taxes;
mixes mixes mixes; fixes fixes fixes; boxes boxes;

expert expert expert; expect expect expect; excels;
exceed exceed exceed; excuse excuse excuse; excels;

Dr. Lux, tax expert, will examine the tax returns.
Dr. Lux, tax expert, will examine the tax returns.

Mr. Cox examined the mixture with extreme care.
Mr. Cox examined the mixture with extreme care.
```

Part 2. Paragraph Practice.

Step 1. Remove all stops.

Step 2. Set Tab Stops: For **Pica** type.................................at 20.
For **Elite** type .........................at 30.

Step 3. Set Line Space Gauge for **double** spacing.

Copy each paragraph **once.**

*Space once after an abbreviation.*

```
     Mr. Roxbury and Mr. Saxton will examine the six
boxes of wax with extreme care.  These boxes were
returned by Prof. Maxton of Knoxville College.

     The Government tax experts were exceedingly
careful in examining the current tax receipts.  The
amount showed an excess of six million dollars over
the previous year.

     Sixteen boxes of explosives were packed with the
most extreme care and shipped by Fox Express Company.
These explosives are to be used in secret experiments
for the U. S. Government.
```

6. **Corrective Work:** (10 Minutes) Make a list of the words in which you find errors; then practice each word 3 times.

7. **Improvement Work:** (10 Minutes) Try another copy of the above 3 paragraphs —for real improvement.

8. **Challenge Work:** (5 Minutes) The following 6 lines test your control of **A Q ; P.** See if you can turn out a **perfect** copy.

```
act ant and ask apt any art all age able acid aged
age all art any ask act add axe ant aged able acid

quit quip quote quite queer queen quack quaint quorum
quip quit quite quote queen queer quail quorum quaint

pin pup put; pull palm pant; pint pile push; punch;
put pin pup; pant pull palm; push pick pile; peper;
```

# LESSON 13

**Aim:** (a) To boost your typing skill by 3-minute timings.

(b) To learn to use Z and / (Slant)

## 1. Machine Adjustments:

(a) Paper Guide: At 0.

(b) Line Space Gauge: For Single Spacing.

(c) Margin Stops:  For **Pica** type........................at 15 and 70.

For **Elite** type........................at 25 and 80.

(d) Top Margin: 10 lines from top edge of paper.

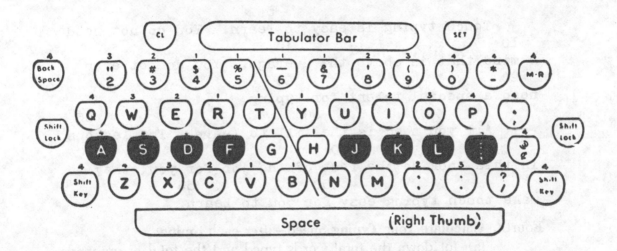

## 2. Warmup: (5 Minutes) Copy the first two lines exactly as shown; then throw the carriage twice and type the sentence ten times.

```
frf juj ftf jyj fgf jhj ded kik sws lol aqa ;p;
fvf jmj fbf jnj dcd k,k sxs l.l dcd k,k sxs l.l

To become an expert typist, you must practice each day.
```

## 3. Skill-Building Work: (20 Minutes) This consists of:

(a) Preview Practice on Words and Phrases................ 5 minutes

(b) Three 3-Minute Timings and Word Practice.............15 minutes

20 minutes

**First: Preview Practice:** To prepare yourself for the 3-minute test, practice each of the following words and phrases three times:

63

REMINDER: When bell rings, finish the word and throw carriage for new line.

```
touch...learn...above...typing...talent...average
special...lessons...you do...for you...is the
do the...of the...in this
```

Second: **Machine Adjustments.**
    (a)  Remove all tab stops.
    (b)  Set a tab stop 5 spaces from your left margin.
    (c)  Set line space gauge for **double** spacing.

Third:   **Three 3-Minute Timings.**
    Time yourself for 3 minutes on the following paragraphs. Repeat them if you finish before the end of 3 minutes.

```
                          5
    Touch typing is easy to learn.  You do not need
  10                        15
a mind that is above the average.  You do not even
  20                          25
need a special talent for typing.
                        30                          35
    All you need is the will to learn.  The lessons
                      40                          45
in this book do the rest of the job for you; they
                      50          53
make touch typing easy for you to learn.
```

Fourth: **Calculate Your Typing Speed—after each timing.**
    (a)  Jot down the total words typed and the total errors made.
    (b)  Subtract 1 for each error from the total words typed.
    (c)  Divide the remainder by 3—because you typed for 3 minutes. The result indicates your typing speed in Correct Words Per Minute.

EXAMPLE: Total Words Typed . . . . . . . . . . . . . . . . . . . . . . . . . 48
             Subtract: (4 Errors x 1) . . . . . . . . . . . . . . . . . . −4
             Correct Words Typed . . . . . . . . . . . . . . . . . . .$3\overline{)44}$
             Correct Words Per Minute . . . . . . . . . . . . . . . 14⅔

Your typing speed in Correct Words is 15 words a minute. Fractions ½ and over are counted as whole numbers.

    (d)  See in which timing you typed the most Correct Words per minute. Consider that your best score.

Assume that the 3 three-minute timings which you have taken show the following results:

| Timing | Correct Words Typed Per Minute |
|---|---|
| 1st...................... | 15 |
| 2nd...................... | 17 |
| 3rd...................... | 16 |

Your best score is in the second timing—because you typed the most Correct Words Per Minute.

REMINDER: After each timing, practice the words in which you made errors.

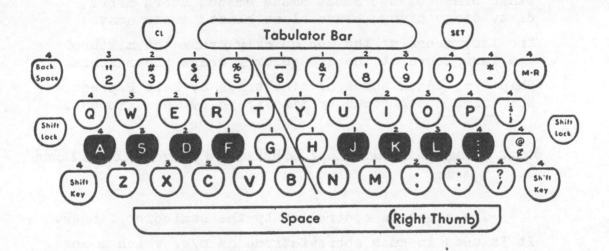

**4. New Key Control:** (10 Minutes) Learning to use New Keys: **Z** **/** (Slant)

       **Z** is controlled by the **A** finger.

      **/** is controlled by the **;** finger.

## Step 1—New Key Preview

Feel the center of each new key—with the fingertip; then return the finger quickly to its home base. Repeat this fingering several times—thinking of the finger and the key it controls—to memorize the New-Key location.

## Step 2—New Key Tryout

*Keep elbows close to body.*
*c/o means care of.*

z z z z aza aza aza aza / / / / ;/; ;/; ;/; ;/;
aza ;/; aza ;/; aza ;/; aza ;/; aza ;/; aza ;/;

### Step 3—Word Drill

```
zip zip zip zip zip zip c/o c/o c/o c/o c/o c/o
zip zip zip zip zip zip c/o c/o c/o c/o c/o c/o
```

5. **Self-Testing Work:** (25 Minutes) Part 1. Words and Sentences. Copy the following 8 lines as shown:

```
zest zest zest; lazy lazy lazy; size size size; zeal;
zero zero zero; zest zest zest; lazy lazy lazy; zeal;

blaze blaze blaze; amaze amaze amaze; zebra zebra;
dizzy dizzy dizzy; blaze blaze blaze; amaze amaze;

The lazy zebra at the zoo quickly drank the mixture.
The lazy zebra at the zoo quickly drank the mixture.

Ship five dozen boxes of zinc trays by Zale Express.
Ship five dozen boxes of zinc trays by Zale Express.
```

Part 2. **Paragraph Practice.** Copy the following 4 paragraphs once. Double spacing.

```
    The slant is controlled by the semicolon finger.
It is used in such abbreviations as n/c, which means
NO CHARGE; and c/o, which means CARE OF.

    If you work with zeal and zest, you will soon be
a competent typist.  The ability to type well is a
very valuable asset.

    You can develop your typing skill quickly by the
proper habits of work.  You should realize that poor
work is a mere waste of time.  Try to be exact.

    Every business firm is dependent on the services
of competent typists.  You are now equipping yourself
with a skill for which there is a constant demand.
```

6. **Corrective Work:** (10 Minutes) Make a list of the words containing errors; then practice each word 3 times.

7. **Challenge Work:** (5 Minutes)  The following 8 lines test your control of **B N V M.** See if you can turn out a **perfect** job.

*Return to guide keys quickly.*

```
bag big bug bit bud bed bid bun bale bend bank bask
but bid bed bun bid big bag bud bask bale band bank

not now nut nor note nose none nude noun nine nest
now not nor nut nose note nude none nine nest next

vim vet van vex vet vast vote veto vase vine vial
van vex vet vim vex vial vine vase veto vote vast

man mix mat mad made mail main make mark mask mine
mad met mix men mask mark made main male made mint
```

# LESSON 14

**Aim:** (a) To boost your typing skill by 4-minute timings.

(b) To learn to use the ? (Question Mark).

## 1. Machine Adjustments:

(a) Paper Guide:  At 0.

(b) Line Space Gauge:  For Single Spacing.

(c) Margin Stops:  For **Pica** type.........................at 15 and 70.

For **Elite** type.........................at 25 and 80.

(d) Top Margin:  10 lines from top edge of paper.

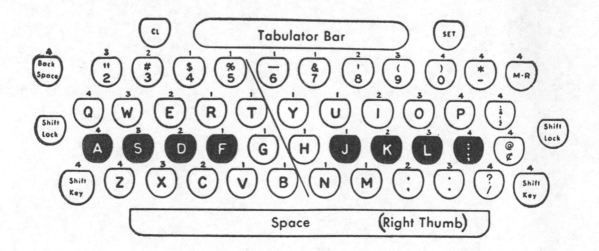

## 2. Warmup: (5 Minutes) Copy the first two lines exactly as shown; then throw the carriage twice and type the sentence ten times.

```
frf juj ftf jyj fgf jhj ded kik sws lol aqa ;p;
fvf jmj fbf jnj dcd k,k sxs l.l aza ;/; aza ;/;
```

```
Liza quickly mixed the very big jar of new soap.
```

## 3. Skill-Building Work: (20 Minutes)

(a) Preview Practice on Words and Phrases................. 3 minutes

(b) Three 4-Minute Timings and Word Practice.............17 minutes

20 minutes

First:  **Preview Practice.** To prepare yourself for the 4-minute timings, practice each of the following words and phrases 3 times:

68

```
touch...learn...above...aside...typing
talent...amount...average...special
lessons...definite...is the...of the
for you...you do...that is...in this
you do not
```

Second: **Machine Adjustments.**
    (a) Remove all tab stops.
    (b) Set a tab stop 5 spaces from your left margin.
    (c) Set line space gauge for **double** spacing.

Third:   **Three 4-Minute Timings.**
    Time yourself for 4 minutes on the following paragraphs, repeating the copy until the end of 4 minutes.

```
                         5
    Touch typing is easy to learn.  You do not need
  10                    15
a mind that is above the average.  You do not even
  20                    25
need a special talent for typing.
                    30                          35
    All you need is the will to learn.  The lessons
                    40                          45
in this book do the rest of the job for you; they
                    50
make touch typing easy for you to learn.
              55                    60
    Try to set aside each day a definite amount of
              65          67
time for each lesson.
```

Fourth:  **Calculate Your Typing Speed—after each timing.**
    (a) Jot down the total words typed and the total errors made.
    (b) Subtract 1 for each error from the total words typed.
    (c) Divide the remainder by 4—because you typed for 4 minutes. The result indicates your typing speed in Correct Words per Minute.

    EXAMPLE: Total Words Typed......................62
               Subtract: (5 Errors x 1).................. −5
               Correct Words Typed...............4/57
               Correct Words Per Minute.................14¼

Your typing speed in correct words is 14 words a minute. Fractions less than ½ are dropped.

(d) See in which timing you typed the most correct words per minute.  Consider that your best score.

> REMINDER: After each timing, practice the words in which you made errors.

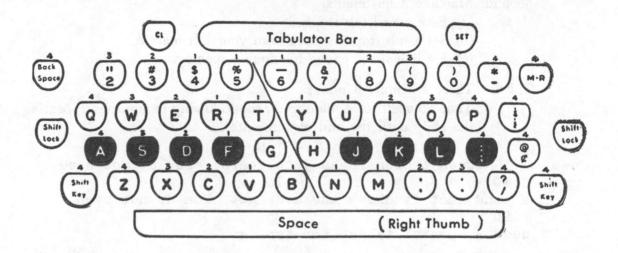

4. **New Key Control:**  (5 Minutes)  Learning to use the Question Mark.  Your right little finger controls the Question Mark.

### Step 1—New Key Preview

1st:  Hold down the left shift key.
2nd:  Reach for the Question Mark key.
3rd:  Return fingers to home base.
4th:  Repeat this several times until you develop smoothness in shifting and reaching for the Question Mark.

### Step 2—New Key Tryout

*Space twice after a Question Mark.*

? ? ? ? ? ? Who?   Who?   Who?   Who?   Who?   Who?
? ? ? ? ? ? Why?   Why?   Why?   Why?   Why?   Why?

5. **Self-Testing Work:**  (30 Minutes)  Part 1.  Sentence Practice.  Copy the following ten lines exactly as shown.

*Keep your eyes on the copy.*
*Every line is different.*

```
How much?   How many?   How soon?   How early?   How fast?
How many?   How much?   How fast?   How large?   How soon?

Where is Max?   Where is Mary?   What is Cora sewing?
Where is Sam?   Where is Paul?   What is Zeke fixing?

Can Max swim?   Can he dance?   Can he play tennis?
Can he dance?   Does he swim?   Do you like tennis?

Did you open the mail?   Did you read the note?
Did you read the note?   Did you open the mail?

Can Van do the work?   Will he require aid?   Who knows?
Can Jim complete it?   Is he quite capable?   Who knows?
```

**Part 2. Paragraph Practice.** Copy the following four paragraphs once. **Double** spacing.

*Space twice after a Question Mark.*
*Throw carriage once after each line.*

```
      Do you set aside a definite amount of time each
day for practice?  Do you start work promptly?  Can
you make the various machine adjustments quickly?
      Do you keep your fingers curved?  Do you strike
each key sharply with the tip of the finger?  Do you
keep your eyes on the copy?
      Do you throw the carriage without looking up?
Do you keep your right hand on the home keys when
you throw the carriage?  Do you use the paper release
to remove your paper?
      Do you practice the words in which you made
errors?  Do you practice them as explained in this
book?  Do you follow the instructions exactly as given?
```

6. **Corrective Work:** (10 Minutes) Make a list of the words in which you find errors; then practice each one until you can type it smoothly and accurately.

7. **Challenge Work:** (5 Minutes) The following four lines test your control of the letters **X** and **Z**. Challenge yourself to turn out **two perfect copies!**

*Think of the finger and the key it controls.*

```
lax vex six tax fix taxed fixing mixing taxing vexing
fix tax vex lax six fixed vexing taxing fixing mixing

zip zoo zest zeal zinc zero lazy zone zoom zinc zealot
zoo zip zoom zone lazy zinc zeal zest zero zone zealot
```

# LESSON 15

**Aim:** (a) To boost your typing skill by 5-minute timings.
(b) To learn to use the figures 1, 4, 7.

## 1. Machine Adjustments:

    (a) Paper Guide: At 0.
    (b) Line Space Gauge: For Single Spacing.
    (c) Margin Stops: For **Pica** type.........................at 15 and 70.
                     For **Elite** type........................at 25 and 80.
    (d) Top Margin: 10 lines from top edge of paper.

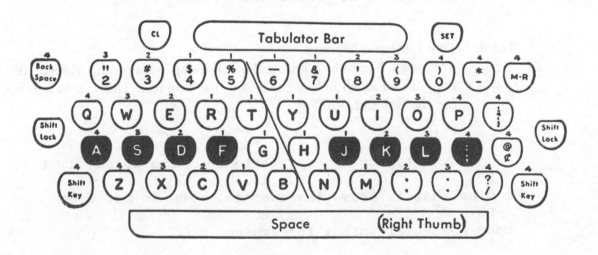

## 2. Warmup:
(5 Minutes) Copy the first two lines exactly as shown; then throw the carriage twice and type the sentence ten times.

```
frf juj ftf jyj fgf jhj ded kik sws lol aqa ;p;
fvf jmj fbf jnj dcd k,k sxs l.l aza ;/; aza ;/;

Pack my box with five dozen jugs of liquid veneer.
```

## 3. Skill-Building Work: (20 Minutes)

    (a) Preview Practice on Words and phrases.................. 3 minutes
    (b) Two 1-Minute Timings and Word Practice.............. 3 minutes
    (c) Two 5-Minute Timings and Word Practice...............14 minutes
                                                    $\overline{20}$ minutes

First:    **Preview Practice.** To prepare yourself for the 1-Minute and 5-Minute Timings, practice each of the following words and phrases **3** times:

```
touch...learn...above...aside...typing
talent...amount...follow...easily...become
typist...average...special...lessons...definite
exactly...quickly...surprised...is the...
of the...in the...in this...for you...
you will...you will be
```

Second:  **Machine Adjustments.**
      (a) Remove all tab stops.
      (b) Set a tab stop 5 spaces from left margin.
      (c) Set line space gauge for **double** spacing.

Third:    **Two 1-Minute Timings.**
      Take two 1-minute tests on the following paragraph. Repeat the copy if you finish before the end of the minute. This is a Warm-up for the 5-minute timing.

```
                              5
    Touch typing is easy to learn.  You do not need
  10                      15
a mind that is above the average.  You do not even
  20                          25  26
need a special talent for typing.
```

Fourth:  **Calculate Your Typing Speed**—after each timing.
      (a) Jot down the total words typed.
      (b) Subtract 1 for each error. The result indicates your typing speed in Correct Words Per Minute.
      (c) See in which timing you typed the most Correct Words. That is your best score. Enter it in your Personal Progress Record of 1-Minute Timings shown in Lesson 9.

Fifth:    **Two 5-Minute Timings.** Relax a while; then take two 5-minute tests on the copy below. Repeat if you finish before end of 5 minutes. Try to maintain your best 1-minute rate.

```
                          5
          Touch typing is easy to learn.  You do not need
   10                        15
a mind that is above the average.  You do not even
   20                        25
need a special talent for typing.
                               30                        35
          All you need is the will to learn.  The lessons
                            40                        45
in this book do the rest of the job for you; they
                       50
make touch typing easy for you to learn.
               55                        60
          Try to set aside each day a definite amount of
               65                        70
time for each lesson.  Follow each step in the lesson
           75                        80
exactly as given.  You will be surprised how easily
           85                        90        92
and quickly you will become a touch typist.
```

Sixth:   **Calculate Your Typing Speed**—after each timing.

(a) Jot down the total words typed and the total errors made.

(b) Subtract 1 for each error from the total words typed.

(c) Divide the remainder by 5—because you typed for 5 minutes. The result shows your typing speed in Correct Words Per Minute.

> EXAMPLE:  Assume that you typed 85 words with 4 errors.
> Total Words Typed . . . . . . . . . . . . . . . . . . . . . .    85
> Subtract (4 Errors x 1) . . . . . . . . . . . . . . . . . . .    −4
> Correct Words Typed . . . . . . . . . . . . . . . 5/81
> Correct Words Per Minute . . . . . . . . . . . .    16½

Your typing speed in Correct Words is 16 words a minute. Fractions less than ½ are dropped.

(d) See in which 5-minute timing you typed the most Correct Words. That is your best score. Keep a Personal Progress Record of your 5-Minute Timings like the following sample. After you finish all 3 timings, enter your best score.

## 5-Minute Timed Typing
### Score Sheet

| Lesson | Correct Words Per Minute |
|--------|--------------------------|
| 15 . . . . . . . . . . . . . . . . . . . . . . . . | 16 |
| 16 . . . . . . . . . . . . . . . . . . . . . . . . | 16 |
| 17 . . . . . . . . . . . . . . . . . . . . . . . . | 18 |

REMINDER:  Practice the words in which you made errors—after each timing.

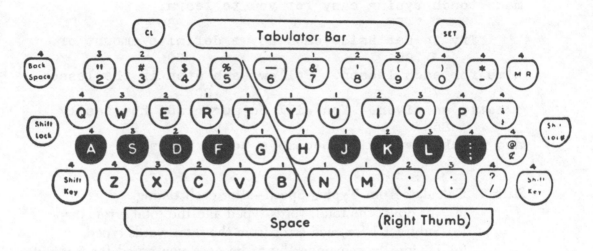

**4. New Key Control:** (10 Minutes) Learning to use figures 1, 4, 7.

Strike small l for the number 1.

Figure **1** is controlled by the **L** finger.

Figure **4** is controlled by the **F** finger.

Figure **7** is controlled by the **J** finger.

### Step 1—New Key Preview

Feel the center of each new key—with the fingertip; then return the finger quickly to its home base.  Repeat this fingering several times—thinking of the finger and the figure key it controls.

### Step 2—New Key Tryout

*Return finger quickly to home base.*

f4f  f4f  f4f  f4f  f4f  f4f  j7j  j7j  j7j  j7j  j7j  j7j
f4f  j7j  f4f  j7j  f4f  j7j  f4f  j7j  f4f  j7j  f4f  j7j

or 4  or 4  or 4  ru 7  ru 7  ru 7  or 4  ru 7  or 4  ru 7
or 4  ru 7  or 4  ru 7  or 4  ru 7  or 4  ru 7  or 4  ru 7

5. **Self-Testing Work:** (25 Minutes) Part 1. Words and Sentences   Copy the following 10 lines exactly as shown:

*Strike small l for the number one. Space once after an abbreviation.*

```
June 1; July 4; April 7; January 4; March 17, 1741
July 4; June 1; March 4; October 7; April 14, 1471

What is the sum of 11 and 7 and 4 and 1 and 714?
What is the sum of 17 and 4 and 7 and 1 and 174?

Florence is 7 years 11 months and 17 days old today.
Veronica is 4 years 11 months and 14 days old today.

Your order of November 14 was shipped on December 17.
Your order of December 11 was shipped on February 14.

Policy No. 141174 will expire on Monday, November 14.
Policy No. 471714 will expire on Friday, December 17.
```

Part 2. Paragraph Practice. **Double spacing.** Copy each paragraph once.

```
     Henry Clay, American statesman and orator, was
born in Hanover County, Virginia, in 1777.
     On June 14, 1777, John Paul Jones became commander
of the American warship, THE RANGER.
     In April 1777, Lafayette landed at night on the
shore of South Carolina to help the colonies.  In July
1777, Congress made Lafayette a general.
     June 14 is now observed as Flag Day because the
flag was adopted by Congress on June 14, 1777.  The
house where Betsy Ross, designer of the flag, lived
is now preserved as a shrine.
```

6. **Corrective Work:** (5 Minutes) As usual.

7. **Improvement Work:** (10 Minutes) Try the first 3 paragraphs again.  See if you can type at least 2 of them **perfect.**

# LESSON 16

**Aim:** (a) To develop sustained typing skill by 5-Minute Timings.

(b) To learn to use the figures **5** and **6**.

## 1. Machine Adjustments:

(a) Paper Guide: At 0.

(b) Line Space Gauge: For Single Spacing.

(c) Margin Stops: For **Pica** type ........................at 15 and 70.

For **Elite** type ........................at 25 and 80.

(d) Top Margin: 10 lines from top edge of paper.

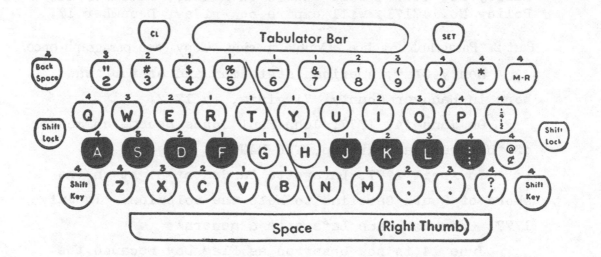

## 2. Warmup: (5 Minutes)
Copy the first two lines exactly as shown; then throw the carriage twice and type the sentence 10 times.

*Strike small l for number one.*

```
frf f4f juj j7j frf f4f juj j7j f4f j7j f4f j7j
1 4 1 7 1 4 1 7 174 4 1 7 1 471 147 471 714 417
```

Queen Anne granted that patent on January 7, 1714.

## 3. Skill-Building Work: (20 Minutes)

(a) Preview Practice on Words and Phrases................ 3 minutes

(b) Two 1-Minute Timings and Word Practice............... 3 minutes

(c) Two 5-Minute Timings and Word Practice.............14 minutes

20 minutes

78

First:     **Preview Practice.**  Practice the following words and phrases 3 times
           each:

```
erase...strike...margin...utmost...typing...
another...correct...teacher...previous...
training...attractive...will be...in your...
in which...You have
```

Second:  **Machine Adjustments.**
           (a) Remove all tab stops.
           (b) Set a tab stop 5 spaces from left margin.
           (c) Set line space gauge for **double** spacing.

Third:     **Two 1-Minute Timings.**  Take two 1-minute tests on the following
           paragraph.  Repeat the copy if you finish before end of minute.
           This is a Warm-up for the 5-minute timing.

```
                              5
    Do not erase.  Do not cross out.  Do not strike
  10                      15
one letter over another.  Let your errors stand.
    20                24
Finish every line you start.
```

Fourth:  (a) Calculate your speed in correct words in each timing.
           (b) Enter the better of the two timings in your Personal Progress
               Record
           (c) Practice the words in which you made errors—after each timing.

Fifth:     **Two 5-Minute Timings.**  Relax a while; then take two 5-minute tim-
           ings on the copy, p. 80.  Repeat if you finish before end of 5 min-
           utes.  Try to maintain your best 1-minute rate.

```
                                 5
        Do not erase.  Do not cross out.  Do not strike
     10                            15
one letter over another.  Let your errors stand.
        20
Finish every line you start.
            25                            30
        You correct your typing errors by practicing the
     35                            40
words in which you made errors.  You have been doing
  45                            50                            55
this in the previous lessons.  Keep right on doing so.
                                 60                       65
That is the best practice for training your fingers
                            70
to strike the right keys.
                                 75
        Try your utmost to turn out attractive work.
     80                            85   86
Take pride in your typing product.
```

Sixth:   (a) Calculate your speed in correct words a minute.

          (b) Enter the better of the two results in your Personal Progress Record.

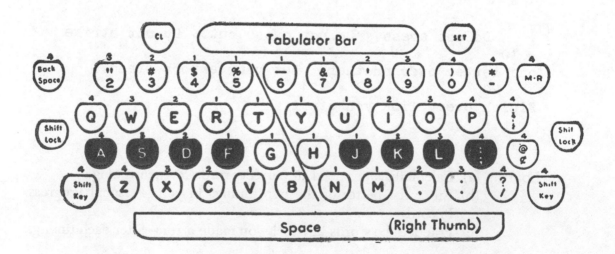

**4. New Key Control:** (10 Minutes) Learning to use the figures 5, 6.

    Figure **5** is controlled by the **F** finger.

    Figure **6** is controlled by the **J** finger.

### Step 1—New Key Preview

Reach and touch the center of each new key—with the fingertip; then return the finger quickly to its home base. Repeat this fingering several times—thinking of the finger and the figure it controls—to memorize the new key location.

### Step 2—New Key Tryout

*Strike sharply. Return finger quickly to home base.*

```
f5f  f5f  f5f  f5f  f5f  f5f  j6j  j6j  j6j  j6j  j6j  j6j
f5f  j6j  f5f  j6j  f5f  j6j  f5f  j6j  f5f  j6j  f5f  j6j

if 5 by 6 if 5 by 6 if 5 by 6 if 5 by 6 if 5 by 6
if 5 by 6 if 5 by 6 if 5 by 6 if 5 by 6 if 5 by 6
```

5. **Self-Testing Work:** (30 Minutes) Part 1. Sentence Practice. Copy the following 12 lines exactly as shown. Single spacing.

*Space once after an abbreviation.*
*Throw carriage twice after every third line.*
*Throw the carriage with a flip of the wrist.*

```
f4f  j7j  f5f  j6j  f4f  j7j  f5f  j6j  f4f  j7j  f5f  j6j
15 lbs. coffee; 16 doz. eggs; 56 boxes oranges;
65 lbs. coffee; 14 doz. eggs; 75 boxes oranges;

or 4 ru 7 it 5 my 6 or 4 ru 7 it 5 my 6 147 156
The Barton Market is at 516 West 147th Street.
The Baxter Market is at 165 East 165th Street.

fr4 ju7 ft5 jy6 f4f  j7j  f5f  j6j  f4f  j7j  f5f  j6j
Robert Fulton was born in Pennsylvania in 1765.
William Penn, English Quaker, was born in 1644.

or 4 ru 7 it 5 by 6 or 4 ru 7 it 5 by 6 174 516
The sum of 15 and 51 and 65 and 41 and 475 is 647.
The sum of 51 and 15 and 56 and 14 and 475 is 611.
```

Part 2.  Paragraph Practice.  **Double** spacing.  Copy each paragraph **once**.

On June 15, 1775, George Washington was elected by Congress the Chief Commander of the American forces. He scored a brilliant victory at Trenton on Christmas night, 1776.

The Declaration of Independence, a famous state paper, was issued by the American Continental Congress on July 4, 1776.  It was drawn up by Thomas Jefferson.

The invasion fleet consisted of 4 battleships, 15 light cruisers, 6 aircraft carriers, 17 troopships, and 5 submarines.  Air protection consisted of 14 bombers, 175 fighters, 6 helicopters, and 75 paratroop planes.

6. **Corrective Work:** (5 Minutes)  Make a list of the words in which you find errors; then practice each word 3 times.

*Thoughtful practice leads to accuracy.*

7. **Challenge Work:** (5 Minutes)  The last paragraph above contains all the figures you have learned so far.  See if you can turn out a **perfect** copy of it.

# LESSON 17

**Aim:** (a) To develop sustained typing skill by 5-minute timings.

(b) To learn to use the figures 3 and 8.

**1. Machine Adjustments:**

(a) Paper Guide: At 0.

(b) Line Space Gauge: For Single Spacing.

(c) Margin Stops: For **Pica** type......................at 15 and 70.

For **Elite** type......................at 25 and 80.

(d) Top Margin: 10 lines from top edge of paper.

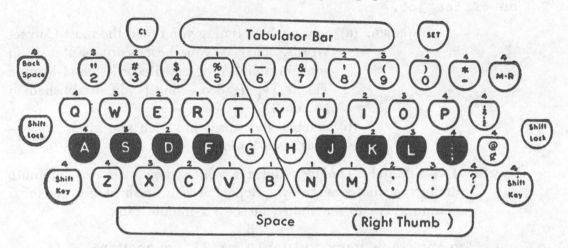

**2. Warmup:** (5 Minutes) Copy the first two lines exactly as shown; then throw the carriage twice and type the sentence 10 times.

```
f4f  j7j  f5f  j6j  f4f  j7j  f5f  j6j  f4f  j7j  f5f  j6j
417  147  517  157  617  167  617  171  714  471  651  174

The sum of 14 and 57 and 67 and 11 and 5 equals 154.
```

**3. Skill-Building Work:** (20 Minutes)

(a) Preview Practice on Words and Phrases................. 3 minutes

(b) Two 1-Minute Timings and Word Practice................. 3 minutes

(c) Two 5-Minute Timings and Word Practice...............14 minutes

$$\overline{\phantom{xxxxx}}$$

20 minutes

First:  **Preview Practice:** Practice each of the following words and phrases 3 times:

```
never...typing...office...become...getting...
acquire...efforts...valuable...personal...
possible...business...shorthand...it is...
it can...to it...in the...to use...to have
if you...from you...why not
```

83

Second: **Machine Adjustments:**
    (a) Remove all tab stops.
    (b) Set a tab stop 5 spaces from left margin.
    (c) Set line space gauge for **double** spacing.

Third:   **Take two 1-minute timings on the following paragraph:**

```
                             5
      Typing is a very valuable skill to acquire.  It
   10                        15                        20
is valuable for personal use and as a means of getting
             25
an office job.
```

REMINDER: (a) See in which timing you typed the most Correct Words. That is your best score. Enter it in your Personal Progress Record—the 1-Minute Timed Typing Score Sheet you established in Lesson 9.

                (b) Practice the words in which you made errors—after each timing.

Fourth: **Two 5-Minute Timings.** Relax a while; then take two 5-minute timings on the copy below. Repeat if you finish before end of 5 minutes. Try to maintain your best 1-minute rate.

```
                             5
      Typing is a very valuable skill to acquire.  It
   10                        15                        20
is valuable for personal use and as a means of getting
                      25                        30
an office job.  This skill is yours to use; it can
             35
never be taken from you.
                             40
      So why not put forth your best efforts to become
   45                        50                        55
a good typist.  You can become a good typist if you
                      60                        65
put your mind to it.  You should also, if possible,
                      70                        75
learn shorthand.  Typing and shorthand are two very
                      80
valuable skills to have.
                             85
      These two skills will help you get a good start
   90                94
in the business world.
```

REMINDER: Enter your best 5-Minute score in your Personal Progress Record.

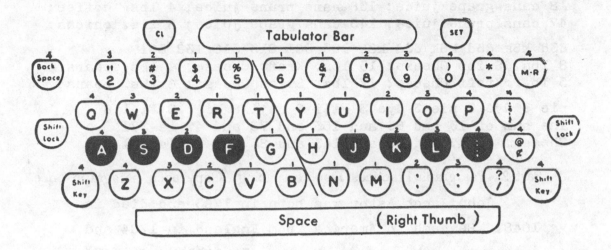

4. **New Key Control:** (10 Minutes) Learning to use the Figures 3 and 8.

Figure 3 is controlled by the **D** finger.
Figure 8 is controlled by the **K** finger.

### Step 1—New Key Preview

Reach and touch the center of each new key—with the fingertip; then return the finger quickly to its home base. Repeat this fingering several times—thinking of the finger and the figure it controls—to memorize the new-key location.

### Step 2—New Key Tryout

*Keep elbows close to body.*

```
d3d k8k d3d k8k d3d k8k d3d k8k d3d k8k d3d k8k
131 313 311 181 818 381 381 381 183 138 318 813

bid 3 bid 3 bid 3 bid 3 oak 8 oak 8 oak 8 oak 8
bid 3 bid 3 bid 3 bid 3 oak 8 oak 8 oak 8 oak 8
```

5. **Self-Testing Work:** (30 Minutes) Part 1. Sentence Practice. Copy the following 12 lines exactly as shown. Single spacing.

*If keys lock press Margin Release.*
*Space once after an abbreviation.*

```
d3d k8k d3d k8k d3d k8k d3d k8k 318 813 138 813 381
13 lbs. lamb roast; 38 lbs. lamb chops; 8 lbs. bananas;
31 lbs. lamb chops; 83 lbs. lamb roast; 3 lbs. peaches;

lie 3 dye 3 pie 3 dye 3 Fiji 8 Fiji 8 Fiji 8
18 cans grape juice; 138 cans prune juice; 4 lbs. coffee;
47 cans prune juice; 143 cans grape juice; 8 lbs. onions;

d3d k8k d3d k8k d3d k8k 183 381 813 318 138 381
8 lbs. Swiss Cheese; 13 lbs. Kraft Cheese; 4 lbs. pears;
5 lbs. Kraft Cheese; 17 lbs. Swiss Cheese; 6 lbs. beans;

pie 3 dye 3 pie 3 dye 3 Fiji 8 Fiji 8 Fiji 8 Fiji 8
The sum of 13 and 83 and 153 and 75 and 47 is 371
The sum of 47 and 75 and 153 and 83 and 13 is 371
```

Part 2. Paragraph Practice. **Double** spacing. Copy each paragraph **once.**

John Jacob Astor was born in 1763 and died in 1848. He came to America from England in 1784 and set up a prosperous fur trade. In 1811 he founded the settlement of Astoria near the mouth of the Columbia River.

Alexander Graham Bell was born in Scotland on March 3, 1847. He invented the telephone in 1876. The Bell Telephone Company was organized in 1877. Mr. Bell also invented the gramophone in 1887.

John Quincy Adams, sixth President of the United States, was born in Massachusetts on July 11, 1767. In 1817 he was appointed Secretary of State. He died in 1848.

Oliver Wendell Holmes, American jurist, was born in Massachusetts on March 8, 1841; graduated from Harvard in 1861; from Harvard Law School in 1866; admitted to the Massachusetts Bar in 1867.

6. **Corrective Work:** (5 Minutes) As usual.

7. **Challenge Work:** (5 Minutes) Select any two of the above paragraphs; then challenge yourself to turn out at least one of them **perfect.**

# LESSON 18

**Aim:** (a) To develop sustained typing skill by 5-Minute Timings.

(b) To learn to use the figures **2** and **9**.

## 1. Machine Adjustments:

(a) Paper Guide:  At 0.

(b) Line Space Gauge:  For Single Spacing.

(c) Margin Stops:  For **Pica** type . . . . . . . . . . . . . . . . . . . . . . . . . . . .at 15 and 70.

For **Elite** type . . . . . . . . . . . . . . . . . . . . . . . . . .at 25 and 80.

(d) Top Margin:  10 lines from top edge of paper.

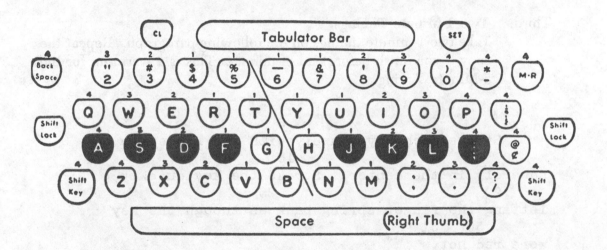

## 2. Warmup:  (5 Minutes)  Copy the first two lines exactly as shown; then throw the carriage twice and type the sentence 10 times.

```
f4f  j7j  f5f  j6j  d3d  k8k  f4f  j7j  f5f  j6j  d3d  k8k
or4  ru7  it5  by6  ie3  ok8  or4  ru7  it5  by6  ie3  ok8
```

The sum of 14 and 16 and 53 and 58 and 174 is 315.

## 3. Skill-Building Work:  (20 Minutes)

(a) Preview Practice on Words and Phrases . . . . . . . . . . . . . . . . 3 minutes

(b) Two 1-Minute Timings and Word Practice . . . . . . . . . . . . . . . 3 minutes

(c) Two 5-Minute Timings and Word Practice . . . . . . . . . . . . . . . .14 minutes

20 minutes

First: **Preview Practice.** Practice each of the following words and phrases 3 times:

```
strike...center...finger...spring...though...
expert...sharply...release...quickly...develop...
letting...squarely...practice...familiar...
fingertip...important...technique...releasing...
instantly...it is...do it...do this...with the...
you get.
```

Second: **Machine Adjustments.**
    (a) Remove all tab stops.
    (b) Set a tab stop 5 spaces from left margin.
    (c) Set line space gauge for **double** spacing.

Third: **Two 1-Minute Timings.**
    Take two 1-minute timings on the following paragraph. Repeat the copy if you finish before end of minute. This is **a warm-up** for the 5-Minute Timing.

```
                                5
    Strike each key sharply with the fingertip and
   10                           15
squarely in the center.  Strike the key quickly,
    20                           25
letting the finger spring back as though the key
      30   31
were red hot.
```

    REMINDER: (a) See in which timing you typed the most Correct Words. That is your best score. Enter it in your Personal Progress Record—the 1-Minute Timed Typing Score Sheet.
         (b) Practice the words in which you made errors—after each timing.

Fourth: **Two 5-Minute Timings.** Relax a while; then take two 5-minute timings on the copy, p. 89. Repeat if you finish before end of 5 minutes. Try to maintain your best 1-minute rate.

5
        Strike each key sharply with the fingertip and
   10                          15
squarely in the center.  Strike the key quickly,
      20                          25
letting the finger spring back as though the key
        30
were red hot.
                         35                          40
        To type fast, it is just as important to release
                    45                          50
the key quickly as it is to strike it quickly.  Expert
               55                          60
typists do this; you too, can do it, with practice.
               05                          70
        One good way to develop this technique is to
               75                          80
practice familiar words and phrases.  Type them over
          85                          90
and over again until you get the knack of hitting the
          95                          100  101
keys quickly and releasing the fingers instantly.

REMINDER: (a) See in which 5-Minute Timing you typed the most Correct Words per minute.  That is your best score.  Enter it in your Personal Progress Record—the 5-Minute Timed Typing Score Sheet which you established in Lesson 15.

(b) Practice the words in which you made errors—after each timing.

4. **New Key Control:** (10 Minutes) Learning to use figures **2** and **9**.
    Figure **2** is controlled by the **S** finger.
    Figure **9** is controlled by the **L** finger.

### Step 1—New Key Preview

Reach and feel the center of each new key—with the fingertip; then return the finger quickly to its home base. Repeat this fingering several times. Think of the finger and the key it controls—to memorize the new key location.

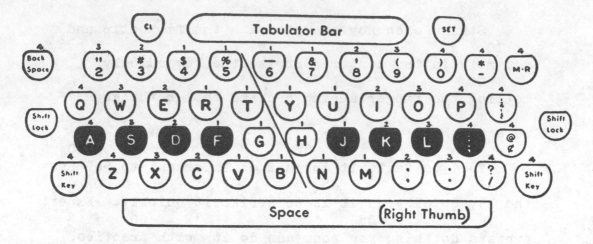

## Step 2—New Key Tryout

*Keep elbows close to body.*

```
s2s  s2s  s2s  s2s  s2s  s2s  191  191  191  191  191  191
s2s  191  s2s  191  s2s  191  s2s  191  s2s  191  s2s  191

bow  2  bow  2  bow  2  bow  2  two  9  two  9  two  9  two  9
bow  2  two  9  bow  2  two  9  bow  2  two  9  bow  2  two  9
```

5. **Self-Testing Work:** (30 Minutes)  Part 1.  Sentence Practice.  Copy the following 12 lines exactly as shown.  Single spacing.

*If keys lock, press Margin Release.*

```
s2s 191 s2s 191 s2s 191 s2s 191 s2s 191 s2s 191 s2s 191
12 lbs. coffee; 19 lbs. Cottage Cheese; 9 lbs. peaches;
19 lbs. apples; 29 lbs. Cheddar Cheese; 2 lbs. bananas;

low 2 fro 9 low 2 fro 9 low 2 fro 9 low 2 fro 9 29 192;
9 lbs. Smoked Tongue; 2 lbs. tomatoes; 9 lbs. avocados;
2 lbs. Cooked Tongue; 9 lbs. avocados; 2 lbs. tomatoes;

s2s 191 s2s 191 219 921 192 s2s 191 s2s 191 291 129
The sum of 29 and 86 and 33 and 92 and 52 is 292.
The sum of 52 and 92 and 86 and 33 and 29 is 292.

ow 2 to 9 ow 2 to 9 we 23 ok 98 we 23 ok 98 s2s 191
George Washington was born on February 22, 1732.
Horatio Alger was born in 1834 and died in 1899.
```

Part 2.  Paragraph Practice.  **Double** spacing.  Copy each paragraph **once.**

*Space once after initials.*

Christopher Latham Sholes was the inventor of the first practical typewriter.  He was born in Columbia County, Pennsylvania, February 14, 1819.

James Monroe, fifth President of The United States, was born on April 28, 1758.  In 1782 he entered politics. In 1799 he was appointed Governor of Virginia.  In 1811 he became Secretary of State; in 1814, Secretary of War; in 1816, President of The United States.

On September 1, 1939, Germany launched undeclared war on Poland.  On September 3, 1939, Great Britain declared war on Germany.  On December 8, 1941, The United States declared war against the Axis.

Samuel F. B. Morse, inventor and artist, was born in 1791 and died in 1872.  In 1829 he went to Europe for three years.  For 12 years he worked on perfecting the electrical telegraph, which was exhibited at New York University in 1837.

6. **Corrective Work:**  (5 Minutes)  As usual.

7. **Challenge Work:**  (5 Minutes)  Try another copy of the above second paragraph. Challenge yourself to a **perfect job.**

# LESSON 19

**Aim:** (a) To develop sustained typing skill by 5-Minute Timings.
(b) To learn to use the Figure **0** and the  -  (Hyphen).

## 1. Machine Adjustments:

(a) Paper Guide:  At 0.
(b) Line Space Gauge:  For Single Spacing.
(c) Margin Stops:  For **Pica** type.........................at 15 and 70.
For **Elite** type.........................at 25 and 80.
(d) Top Margin:  10 lines from top edge of paper.

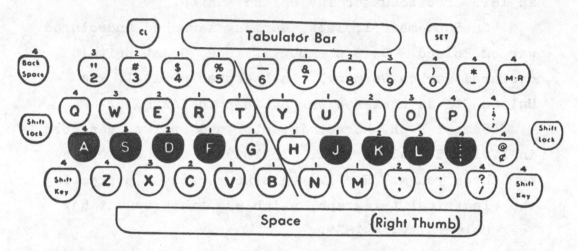

## 2. Warmup:

(5 Minutes)  Copy the first two lines exactly as shown; then throw the carriage twice and type the sentence 10 times.

```
f4f  j7j  f5f  j6j  d3d  k8k  s2s  191  f4f  j7j  f5f  j6j
s2s  191  d3d  k8k  f4f  j7j  f5f  j6j  f4f  j7j  f5f  j6j
```

The sum of 47 and 65 and 38 and 92 and 16 equals 258.

## 3. Skill-Building Work:  (20 Minutes)

(a) Preview Practice on Words and Phrases ................. 3 minutes
(b) Two 1-Minute Timings and Word Practice............... 3 minutes
(c) Two 5-Minute Timings and Word Practice...............14 minutes
                                                          _____
                                                          20 minutes

First:  **Preview Practice.**  Each word and phrase 3 times:

```
expert...typing...margin...always...before...
permits...others...reached...equipped...machines...
carriage...typewriter...approaching...you are...
of the...for the...on the...you may...before the
```

92

**Second: Machine Adjustments for Timed Typing.**
      (a) Remove all tab stops.
      (b) Set a tab stop 5 spaces from left margin.
      (c) Set line space gauge for **double** spacing.

**Third: Two 1-Minute Timings.**
```
                          5
     Your typewriter is equipped with a bell which
  10                            15
rings to warn you that you are approaching the end
     20    21
of the line.
```

      REMINDER: Score the better of the two 1-Minute timings. Try
           to maintain that rate on the 5-Minute timings.

**Fourth: Two 5-Minute Timings.**
```
                          5
     Your typewriter is equipped with a bell which
  10                            15
rings to warn you that you are approaching the end
     20
of the line.
               25                            30
     On some machines, the bell rings five spaces
                    35                            40
before the margin stop is reached; on other machines,
                     45                            50
it rings when there are six or seven spaces left.
                    55
     The ring of the bell permits you to keep your
  60                       65
eyes on the copy.  When you hear the bell, finish
  70                            75
the word you are typing and throw the carriage for
  80
the next line.
                    85                            90
     Do not look up to watch for the end of the line;
               95                            100
you may lose your place in the copy.  Always keep
               105                            110
your eyes on the copy like the expert typist.
```

      REMINDER: (a) Score the better of the two 5-Minute timings.
             (b) Enter the result in your Personal Progress Record.

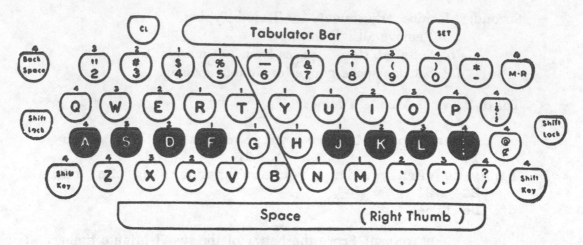

**4. New Key Control:** (10 Minutes) Learning to use Figure **0** and **-** (Hyphen)

**0** is controlled by the **semicolon** finger.

**-** is controlled by the **semicolon** finger.

## Step 1—New Key Preview

Reach and touch the center of each new key—with the fingertip; then return the finger quickly to its home base. Repeat this fingering several times. Think of the finger and the key it controls—to memorize new-key location.

## Step 2—New Key Tryout

```
;0; ;0; ;0; ;0; ;0; ;0; ;-; ;-; ;-; ;-; ;-; ;-;
;0; ;-; ;0; ;-; ;0; ;-; ;0; ;-; ;0; ;-; ;0; ;-;

10-room; 10-room; 10-room; 10-room; 10-room;
20-room; 20-room; 20-room; 20-room; 20-room;
```

**5. Self-Testing Work:** (30 Minutes) Part 1. Sentence Practice. Copy the following 12 lines exactly as shown. Single spacing.

*Space once after semicolon.*
*Space twice after colon.*
*Strike two hyphens -- without spacing -- for a dash.*

```
f4f j7j f5f j6j d3d k8k s2s 191 ;0; ;-; ;0; ;-;
one-half; one-fourth; one-eighth; three-quarters;
one-half; two-thirds; one-fourth; three-sevenths;

f4f j7j f5f j6j d3d k8k s2s 191 ;0; ;-; ;0; ;-;
20-room house; 30-room house; 40-room house;
50-room house; 60-room house; 70-room house;

f4f j7j f5f j6j d3d k8k s2s 191 ;0; ;-; ;0; ;-;
One-fourth may be typewritten like this:  1/4.
One-eighth may be typewritten like this:  1/8.
```

```
f4f j7j f5f j6j d3d k8k s2s 191 ;0; ;-; ;0; ;-;
Every expert was once a beginner--with ambition.
Every expert was once a beginner--with ambition.
```

Part 2. Paragraph Practice. **Double** spacing. Copy each paragraph **once**.

> *Do not space before or after the hyphen.*
> *Do not space before or after the comma in figures.*

As you have seen in the above sentence practice, the hyphen is used for typing compound words. Here are a few more examples: up-to-date, first-class, by-product.

The hyphen is used also to divide words between syllables at the end of a line. When the bell rings, finish the word if it is short--less than six letters. If the word is longer, divide it at the end of a syllable.

The hyphens in the following words show where they could be divided at the end of a line: after-noon, state-ment, hesi-tate, cer-ti-fi-cate, exami-na-tion.

The sum of 10 and 20 and 30 and 40 and 50 and 60 and 70 and 80 and 90 and 100 and 105 and 106 and 107 and 108 and 109 and 110 equals 1,195.

6. **Corrective Work:** (5 Minutes) As usual.

7. **Challenge Work:** (5 Minutes) Here is a new paragraph. Challenge yourself to turn out a **perfect** copy—on the first trial:

> *Do not space after the first initial in a.m. and p.m.*

Have you seen the new 7-room house at 175 West 239th Street? It is equipped with every up-to-date, labor-saving device for the home. You may inspect it free of charge any day except Sunday between 10 a.m. and 4 p.m.

# LESSON 20

**Aim:** (a) To develop sustained typing skill by 5-Minute Timings.
(b) To learn to use the keys: ¢ (Cents) and ½ (One-Half)

**1. Machine Adjustments:**
  (a) Paper Guide:  At 0.
  (b) Line Space Gauge:  For Single Spacing.
  (c) Margin Stops:  For **Pica** type.........................at 15 and 70.
                    For **Elite** type.........................at 25 and 80.
  (d) Top Margin:  10 lines from top edge of paper.

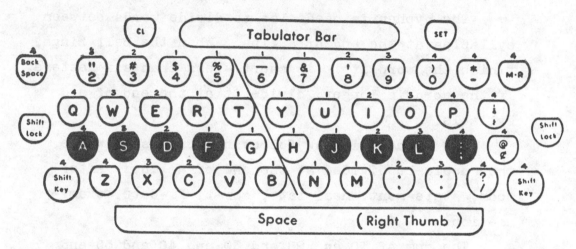

**2. Warmup:** (5 Minutes) Copy the first two lines exactly as shown; then throw
the carriage twice and type the sentence 10 times:

```
f4f j7j f5f j6j d3d k8k s2s 191 ;0; ;-; ;0; ;-;
s2s 191 ;0; ;-; d3d k8k f4f j7j ;0; ;-; ;0; ;-;
```

Max Zale made a long-distance flight of 2,590 miles.

**3. Skill-Building Work:** (20 Minutes)
  (a) Preview Practice on Words and Phrases ................. 3 minutes
  (b) Two 1-Minute Timings and Word Practice............... 3 minutes
  (c) Two 5-Minute Timings and Word Practice.................14 minutes
                                                          ――――――――
                                                          20 minutes

First:    **Preview Practice.** Each word and phrase 3 times:

```
called...fourth...typing...letter...always...
capital...holding...depress...fingers...release...
touching...slightly...position...right-hand...of the
for the...all the...with the...you have
```

**Second: Machine Adjustments for Timed Typing.**
      (a) Remove all tab stops.
      (b) Set a tab stop 5 spaces from left margin.
      (c) Set line space gauge for **double** spacing.

**Third: Two 1-Minute Timings.**

```
                            5
    You type capital letters by holding down a key
 10                         15                      20
called the shift key while you strike the letter key.
```

        REMINDER: (a) Score the better of the two 1-Minute Timings.
                    (b) Try to maintain that rate on the 5-Minute Timings.

**Fourth: Two 5-Minute Timings.**

```
                            5
    You type capital letters by holding down a key
 10                         15
called the shift key while you strike the letter key.
    20                          25
    There are two shift keys.  Hold down the left
    30                          35
shift key for typing right-hand capitals; hold down
    40                          45
the right shift key for typing left-hand capitals.
    50                          55
Always use the fourth finger for the shift key.
        60                              65
    Keep your wrists low but not touching the frame
        70                              75
of the machine.  Raise the other fingers slightly as
        80                              85
you depress the shift key with the fourth finger.
            90                              95
    Be sure that you hold the shift key all the way
        100                             105
down until you have struck the letter key; then re-
        110                     115         117
lease the shift key and return finger to home base.
```

        REMINDER: (a) Score the better of the two 5-Minute Timings.
                    (b) Enter the result in your Personal Progress Record.

TYPING TIP: *If you are making more than 5 errors in a 5-Minute Timing, slow down a bit. Type with better control of your finger movements. Typing speed alone is not enough; accuracy is just as important.*

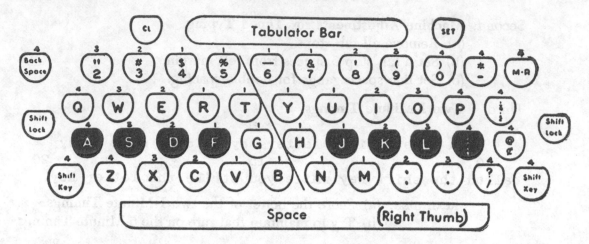

4. **New Key Control:** (10 Minutes) Learning to use ¢ and ½.
     ¢ is controlled by the **little** finger.
     ½ is controlled by the **little** finger.

### Step 1—New Key Preview

Reach and touch the center of each new key—with the fingertip; then return the finger quickly to home base. Repeat this fingering several times. Think of the finger and the key it controls. Memorize the new-key location.

### Step 2—New Key Tryout

*Strike hard. Keep elbows close to body.*

¢ ¢ ¢ ¢  ;¢;  ;¢;  ;¢;  ;¢;  ½ ½ ½ ½  ;½;  ;½;  ;½;  ;½;
;¢;  ;½;  ;¢;  ;½;  ;¢;  ;½;  ;¢;  ;½;  ;¢;  ;½;  ;¢;  ;½;

10½¢  10½¢  10½¢  10½¢  10½¢  12½¢  12½¢  12½¢  12½¢
13½¢  13½¢  13½¢  13½¢  13½¢  19½¢  19½¢  19½¢  19½¢

5. **Self-Testing Work:** (30 Minutes) Part 1. Sentence Practice. Copy the following 12 lines exactly as shown. Single spacing. Throw carriage twice after every third line.

*Space once after a semicolon.*

;/;  ;¢;  ;½;  ;-;  ;/;  ;¢;  ;½;  ;-;  ;/;  ;¢;  ;½;  ;-;
Chuck Steak 39¢; Round Roast 78¢; Ribs of Beef 70¢;
Round Roast 78¢; Chuck Steak 39¢; Legs of Lamb 37¢;

;/;  ;¢;  ;½;  ;-;  ;/;  ;¢;  ;½;  ;-;  ;/;  ;¢;  ;½;  ;-;
Soap 12¢; Spry 33¢; Corn 34¢; Figs 25¢; Beans 14¢;
Figs 25¢; Corn 34¢; Spry 33¢; Soap 12¢; Bread 26¢;

*Space twice after period at end of sentence.*

**Second: Machine Adjustments for Timed Typing.**

    (a) Remove all tab stops.

    (b) Set a tab stop 5 spaces from left margin.

    (c) Set line space gauge for **double** spacing.

**Third:　Two 1-Minute Timings.**

```
                            5
      The backspace key is one of the most useful
     10                      15
time-saving devices on your typewriter.  You use
        20                        25
it to back up a space, or to darken a light
            29
impression.
```

      REMINDER:　(a) Score the better of the two 1-Minute Timings.

                 (b) Try to maintain that rate on the 5-Minute Timings.

**Fourth: Two 5-Minute Timings.**

```
                            5
      The backspace key is one of the most useful time-
10                    15                      20
saving devices on your typewriter.  You use it to back
                  25                      30
up a space, to darken a light impression, or to pivot.
              35                        40
To pivot means to type a line so that the last letter
              45                    50
is at the right margin or other chosen point.
                  55                      60
      For example, if you want a date line to end at
                  65                      70
the right margin, place the carriage with the printing
              75                      80
point indicator at the right margin and backspace once
              85
for each stroke in the date line.
      90                      95
      The most important use of the backspace key is in
      100        103
centering words or lines.
```

      REMINDER:　(a) Score the better of the two 5-Minute timings.

                 (b) Enter the result in your Personal Progress Record.

---

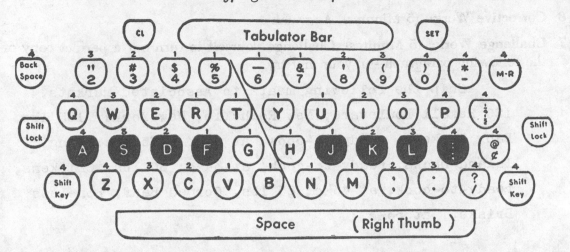

```
;/; ;¢; ;½; ;-; ;/; ;¢; ;½; ;-; ;/; ;¢; ;½; ;-;
Size 13½ shirt is too small.  Purchase size 15½.
Size 12½ socks is too large.  Purchase size 10½.

;/; ;¢; ;½; ;-; ;/; ;¢; ;½; ;-; ;/; ;¢; ;½; ;-;
Ship 170 notebooks at 9½¢ and 6 doz. pencils at 58¢.
Ship 190 notebooks at 8½¢ and 5 doz. pencils at 34¢.
```

Part 2. Paragraph Practice. **Double** spacing. Copy each paragraph once.

*Space once after an abbreviation.*
*Space twice after a colon.*

```
      Prepare a bill for the following items:  29 lbs.
butter at 89½¢; 36 doz. eggs at 69½¢; 28 doz. oranges
at 57½¢; 15 bu. potatoes at 79½¢.

      Our company ordered 15 Ajax Pencil Sharpeners at
98¢; 6 doz. Circular Rubber Erasers at 43½¢; 24 No. 68
Spiral Stenographic Notebooks at 7½¢.

      Deliver the following order to Mrs. Beverly
Vinson at 390 West 135th Street, New York City:  2 lbs.
Temple Oranges at 13½¢; 3 lbs. Red Circle Coffee at
91¢; 2 lbs. Lima Beans at 29¢.

      The Johnston Hardware Company, Toledo, Ohio has
ordered the following supplies:  15 Pruning Shears,
10-inch, at 79½¢; 24 Steel Rakes, 14-inch, at 81½¢;
16 Steel Spades, D-Handle, at 93½¢.
```

6. **Corrective Work:** (5 Minutes)  As usual.

7. **Challenge Work:** (5 Minutes)  Challenge yourself to turn out a **perfect** copy of the following paragraph—on your first try:

```
        Ship the following meats to Associated Markets,
120 Rexall Boulevard, New Rochelle, New York:  135 lbs.
Baby Turkeys, ready-to-cook, at 42½¢; 175 lbs. Long
Island Ducks, ready-to-cook, at 34½¢; 60 lbs. Chickens,
ready-to-cook, at 43½¢; 85 lbs. Corned Beef, Boneless
Brisket, at 53½¢.
```

## LESSON 21

**Aim:** (a)  To develop sustained typing skill by 5-Minute Timings.
(b)  To learn **Horizontal Centering** (Equal Left and Right Margins).

1. **Machine Adjustments:**
   (a)  Paper Guide:  At 0.
   (b)  Line Space Gauge:  For Single Spacing.
   (c)  Margin Stops:  For Pica type.........................at 15 and 70.
   For Elite type.........................at 25 and 80.
   (d)  Top Margin:  10 lines from top edge of paper.

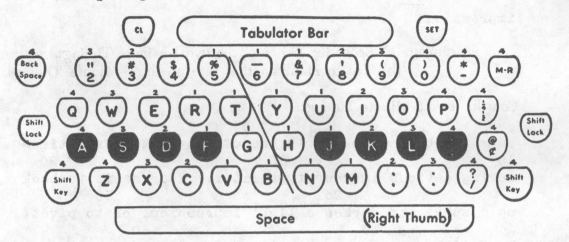

2 **Warmup:** (5 Minutes)  Copy the first two lines exactly as shown; then throw the carriage twice and type the sentence 10 times.

```
f4f j7j f5f j6j d3d k8k s2s 191 ;0; ;-; 191 ;0; ;-;
;/; ;¢; ;½; ;-; ;/; ;¢; ;½; ;-; ;/; ;¢; ;½; ;-; ;¢;
```

The basic per-hour rate of 75½¢ was raised to 89½¢.

3. **Skill-Building Work:** (20 Minutes)
   (a)  Preview Practice on Words and Phrases.................. 3 minutes
   (b)  Two 1-Minute Timings and Word Practice. ............. 3 minutes
   (c)  Two 5-Minute Timings and Word Practice...............14 minutes
   _____
   20 minutes

**First:**  **Preview Practice.** Each word and phrase 3 times.

```
useful...number...devices...example...machine...
carriage...printing...midpoint...backspace...
whichever...indicator...typewriter...impression...
centering...time-saving...of the...at the...in the...
if you...you have...from the...on your
```

4. **New Work:** (15 Minutes) Learning Horizontal Centering.
Horizontal centering means typing material across the paper so that the left and right margins are equal.

To center horizontally: (a) Set the carriage at the center—42 for Pica type; 50 for Elite type.

(b) Backspace once for each two strokes in the material to be centered. If one letter is left over, ignore it.

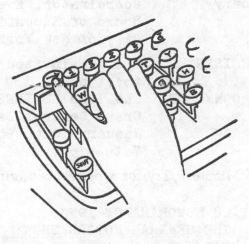

Fig. 17. Location of Backspace Key.
Some Typewriters Show an Arrow.

**New Work Tryout:** A. To center the word INDEPENDENCE
1. Set carriage at center (42 or 50).
2. Backspace **once** for each two strokes as you say, IN DE PE ND EN CE
3. Type the word.

B To center the word EDUCATION
1. Set carriage at center (42 or 50).
2. Backspace **once** for each two strokes as you say, ED UC AT IO (Disregard N).
3. Type the word.

C. To center the name FRANKLIN D. ROOSEVELT
1. Set carriage at center (42 or 50).
2. Backspace **once** for each two strokes as you say, FR AN KL IN Space D Period Space RO OS EV EL (Disregard T)
3. Type the name.

5. **Self-Testing Work:** (30 Minutes) Now test your knowledge of horizontal centering. Center each of the following lines. Single space. Throw carriage twice after each group.

George Washington
Sir Winston Churchill
James Madison
Andrew Jackson

THE POWER OF POSITIVE THINKING
FOR YOUNG PEOPLE
by
Norman Vincent Peale

Dr. Albert Schweitzer
Medical Missionary
Philosopher
Man of God

Samuel Schenberg
Coordinator, Evening High Schools
Board of Education
City of New York

GRADUATION EXERCISES
at
HIGH SCHOOL OF COMMERCE
will be held
on
June 16, 1954

You are Invited
to attend
The 1956 BUSINESS SHOW
Grand Central Palace
January 19 to 25
7 to 9 p.m.

6. **Challenge Work:** (5 Minutes) Try for a **perfect** centering job of these two advertisements:

GM MOTORAMA OF 1956
THE GENERAL MOTORS SHOW
Waldorf-Astoria
Week of January 16
Admission Free
Bring a Friend

DINE OUT TONIGHT
at one of these
BETTER PLACES
China Bowl
Little Vienna
Little Hungary

# LESSON 22

<u>Aim:</u> (a) To develop sustained typing skill by 5-Minute Timings.
(b) To learn **Vertical Centering** (Equal Top and Bottom Margins).

## 1. Machine Adjustments:
(a) Paper Guide:  At 0.
(b) Line Space Gauge:  For Single Spacing.
(c) Margin Stops:  For **Pica** type......................................at 15 and 70.
For **Elite** type...........................at 25 and 80.
(d) Top Margin:  10 lines from top edge of paper.

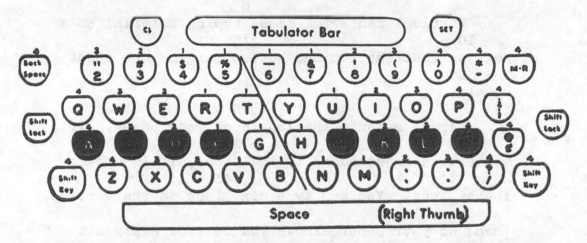

## 2. Warmup: (5 Minutes) Copy the first two lines exactly as shown; then throw the carriage twice and type the sentence 10 times.

```
f4f j7j f5f j6j d3d k8k s2s 191 ;0; ;-; 191 ;0; ;-;
;/; ;¢; ;½; ;-; ;/; ;¢; ;½; ;-; s2s 191 d3d k8k ;¢;
```

Ship at once 165 pads, 370 books, and 248 pencils.

## 3. Skill-Building Work: (20 Minutes)
(a) Preview Practice on Words and Phrases........................ 3 minutes
(b) Two 1-Minute Timings and Word Practice................... 3 minutes
(c) Two 5-Minute Timings and Word Practice.................14 minutes
                                                                    ―――――
                                                                    20 minutes

First:    **Preview Practice.** Each word and phrase 3 times.

equal...bottom...number...eleven...vertical...
subtract...centering...sixty-six...available...
remainder...it is...in the...of your...so that...
from the

Second: **Machine Adjustments for Timed Typing.**
      (a) Remove all tab stops.
      (b) Set a tab stop 5 spaces from left margin.
      (c) Set line space gauge for **double** spacing.

Third:   **Two 1-Minute Timings.**

```
                           5
    Vertical centering means typing material on a
    10                            15
page so that the top and bottom margins are about
    20
equal.
```

Fourth: **Two 5-Minute Timings.**

```
                           5
    Vertical centering means typing material on a
    10                            15
page so that the top and bottom margins are about
    20
equal.
                                   25
    First, measure the length of your paper.  If
    30                            35
you are using standard typing paper, it is eleven
      40                            45
inches long.  You can type six lines to the vertical
    50                            55
inch; so your paper allows you to type sixty-six
        60
lines from top to bottom.
            65                                70
    To center vertically, count the lines and spaces
        75                            80
in the material to be centered.  Subtract that number
    85                            90
from sixty-six, which is the total number of lines
    95
available on the paper.
                100                            105
    Divide the remainder by two, to get the number
        110                            115
of lines from the top edge on which the typing should
    119
start.
```

4. **New Work:** (15 Minutes) Learning Vertical Centering. Vertical centering means typing material on a page so that the top and bottom margins are about equal.

To center material vertically (from top to bottom):

(a) Count the typewritten lines and blank lines in the material to be centered. Jot down the total.

(b) Subtract the total from 66, which is the number of typing lines on a full sheet of standard typing paper. For a half sheet, subtract from 33. The remainder is the number of single spaces left for top and bottom margins.

(c) Divide the remainder by 2. This gives you the number of spaces from the top edge for your starting point. Disregard fractions.

> EXAMPLE: To center 25 lines (typewritten and blank) on a full sheet, subtract 25 from 66 ..................................................... 66
> Lines Required ................................................ −25
> Lines left for top and bottom margins ..................... 41
> Divide 41 in half: 41 ÷ 2 = 20½
> Start typing on line 20 from top edge of paper.

**New Work Tryout:** Center the following advertisement on a full sheet:

ACME MARKET
Money—Saving Buys
BEEF ROUND ROAST
69¢ lb.

FRANKFURTERS
53¢ lb.

SMOKED TONGUE
48¢ lb.

SIRLOIN STEAK
82¢ lb.

Follow these steps:

1. Count the typewritten lines (10)
2. Count the blank lines between the typewritten lines (4)
3. Add the typewritten lines and the blank lines (14)
4. Subtract 14 lines from the total number of lines which the paper accommodates: 66 minus 14 equals 52.
5. Divide 52 by 2; Result: 26.
6. Single space 26 times from top edge of the paper.
7. Set the carriage at the center—42 for Pica; 50 for Elite.
8. Center the first line ACME MARKET
9. Single space and center: Money-Saving Buys
10. Double space and center: BEEF ROUND ROAST

    NOTE: Follow the above steps until you have centered the last line: 82¢ lb.

5. **Self-Testing Work:** (30 Minutes) Center horizontally and vertically each of the following 2 advertisements on a full sheet.

> REMINDER: (a) You can type 6 lines to the vertical inch.
>
>          (b) Standard typing paper is 11 inches long; so it allows you to type 66 lines (6 x 11) from top to bottom.

(1)   BASEBALL GAME

      High School of Commerce
      Vs.
      De Witt Clinton High School

      May 18, 1954

      at

      EBBETTS FIELD

      Game Starts at 2:30
      Bring a Friend

(2)   EXCITING TOURS

      To

      THE ORIENT
      and
      THE THOUSAND ISLANDS

      Arranged by

      WONDER-TOURS COMPANY
      615 Zerega Avenue
      Chicago 15, Illinois

Center No. 3 and No. 4, each on a half sheet.

> REMINDER: (a) A half sheet allows you to type 33 lines.
>
>          (b) Subtract the total number of typewritten and blank lines from 33; then divide by 2—to give you the number of spaces from the top edge for your starting point.

(3)   THIS BOOK

      is
      from

      THE LIBRARY

      of

      JAMES MONROE HIGH SCHOOL
      New York City

(4)   MOTOR BOAT SHOW

      Now At

      KINGSBRIDGE ARMORY

      January 15-23

      Admission 75¢

      3 p.m. to 9:30 p.m.

**6. Challenge Work:** (5 Minutes) Try for **a perfect** centering job of the following advertisement on a full sheet:

ADULT EDUCATION

Hunter College
School of Education
Park Avenue at 69th Street

EVENING COURSES
for
Men and Women

15-Week Term

Beginning
February 10

REGISTER NOW

# LESSON 23

**Aim:** (a) To develop sustained typing skill by 5-Minute Timings.
(b) To learn to use the keys: $ (Dollars) and & (Ampersand).

1. **Machine Adjustments:**
   (a) Paper Guide:  At 0.
   (b) Line Space Gauge:  For Single Spacing.
   (c) Margin Stops:  For **Pica** type.........................at 15 and 70.
                          For **Elite** type.........................at 25 and 80.
   (d) Top Margin:  10 lines from top edge of paper.

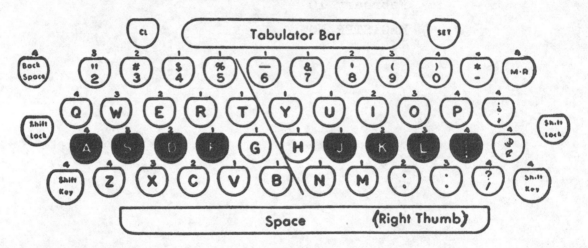

2. **Warmup:** (5 Minutes) Copy the first two lines exactly as shown; then throw the carriage twice and type the sentence 10 times.

```
f4f j7j f5f j6j d3d k8k s2s l9l ;0; ;-; l9l ;0; ;-;
;/; ;¢; ;½; ;/; ;¢; ;½; d3d k8k s2s l9l ;/; ;¢; ;½;
```

The fraction one-half may be typewritten as ½ or 1/2.

3. **Skill-Building Work:** (20 Minutes)
   (a) Preview Practice on Words and Phrases.................. 3 minutes
   (b) Two 1-Minute Timings and Word Practice................ 3 minutes
   (c) Two 5-Minute Timings and Word Practice............14 minutes
                                                          ─────────
                                                          20 minutes

First:    **Preview Practice.** Each word and phrase 3 times:

```
cannot...margin...typing...device...enough...
before...spaces...enables...located...releases...
machines...typewriter...at the...you are...on the...
and the...it is...you have...on which
```
110

**Second: Machine Adjustments for Timed Typing.**
    (a) Clear all tab stops.
    (b) Set a tab stop 5 spaces from left margin.
    (c) Set line space gauge for **double** spacing.

**Third:  Two 1-Minute Timings.**

```
                              5
     Your typewriter has a key that releases the
        10                      15
margin lock and enables you to finish a word at the
        20    21
end of a line.
```

**Fourth:  Two 5-Minute Timings.**

```
                              5
     Your typewriter has a key that releases the
        10                      15
margin lock and enables you to finish a word at the
        20
end of a line.
                         25                        30
     If you are typing a long word that cannot be
                      35                          40
divided and the margin locks before you complete the
                      45                        50
word, depress the margin release key.  This will en-
                   55
able you to finish the word.
                     60                          65
     On some machines, the margin release key is
                   70                          75
located on the right side; on other machines, it is
                   80
located on the left side.
                         85
     When the typewriter bell rings, it means that
90                      95                        100
you have about seven spaces left before the keys lock.
                      105                        110
In most cases, when the bell rings, you will have
                   115              118
enough spaces left to finish the word.
```

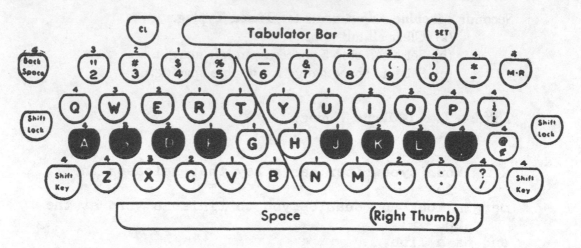

**4. New Key Control:** (10 Minutes) Learning to use **$ &**
   **$** is controlled by the **F** finger. Use right shift key.
   **&** is controlled by the **J** finger. Use left shift key.

### Step 1—New Key Preview

Using the shift key, reach and touch the center of each new key; then return fingers quickly to home base. Practice it this way—Shift, Reach, Return . . . until you can do it smoothly. Think of the finger and the new key it controls.

### Step 2—New Key Tryout

f$f  f$f  f$f  f$f  f$f  f$f  j&j  j&j  j&j  j&j  j&j  j&j
f$j  j&j  f$f  j&j  f$f  j&j  f$f  j&j  f$f  j&j  f$f  j&j

Hats, $4; Hats, $4; Hats, $4; Hats, $4; Hats, $4;
Dix & Co. Dix & Co. Dix & Co. Dix & Co. Dix & Co.

5. **Self-Testing Work:** (30 Minutes) Part 1. Sentence Practice. Copy the following 12 lines exactly as shown. Single spacing.

*Space once after an abbreviation.*

```
f$f j&j f$f j&j f$f j&j f$f j&j f$f j&j f$f j&j
Tickets, $5 each; Tickets, $5 each; Tickets, $5 each;
Zuckor & Company; Zuckor & Company; Zuckor & Company;

f$f j&j f$f j&j f$f j&j f$f j&j f$f j&j f$f j&j
Mintz & Co. offers 1952 Cadillac cars at $2,120.
Dixon & Co. offers 1953 Chrysler cars at $1,975.

f$f j&j f$f j&j f$f j&j f$f j&j f$f j&j f$f j&j
Fly to Miami non-stop in 3 hrs., 45 min. for $45.
Fly to Tampa non-stop in 3 hrs., 10 min. for $41.

f$f j&j f$f j&j f$f j&j f$f j&j f$f j&j f$f j&j
Carter & Co. offer Bendix Washing Machines at $140.
Parker & Co. offer Maytag Washing Machines at $157.
```

Part 2. Paragraph Practice. **Double** spacing. Copy each paragraph once.

```
     Crane & Co. are going out of business on May 28.
To clear out their entire stock, they offer Tropical
Worsted Suits, formerly sold at $53, at the money-
saving price of $49.75.
     Mail a statement to each of the following firms
showing the amount due:  Jones & Manson, $130.75;
Van Duzen & Bradley, $420; Charles & Byers, $168.90;
Hoe & Sons, $123.50.
     De Voux & Co., fashion designers, offer Designer
Coats, formerly $90.85, at the money-saving price of
$75.50.  They offer also Cocktail Gowns, formerly
$49.75, at the money-saving price of $37.95.
```

6. **Corrective Work:** (5 Minutes) As usual.

**7. Challenge Work:** (5 Minutes) Challenge yourself to turn out a perfect copy of the following paragraph:

> REMINDER: (a) Strike two hyphens -- without spacing -- for a dash.
> (b) Space once after the period in an abbreviation.

        Smith & Co. offer Foam Cushion Chairs at $31.50--
a saving of $5.50.  Brooks & Co. offer Wrought Iron
Tables at $12.95--a saving of $3.75.  Wilkins & Co.
offer Double-Track Storm Windows and Screen at $9.95--
a saving of $2.90.

# LESSON 24

**Aim:** (a) To develop sustained typing skill by 5-Minute Timings.
(b) To learn to use % (Per Cent) and _ (Underscore) keys.

## 1. Machine Adjustments:
(a) Paper Guide: At 0.
(b) Line Space Gauge: For Single Spacing.
(c) Margin Stops: For **Pica** type.........................at 15 and 70.
For **Elite** type.........................at 25 and 80.
(d) Top Margin: 10 lines from top edge of paper.

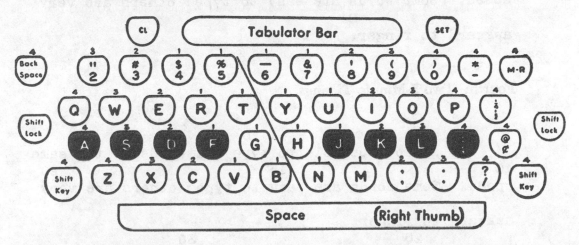

## 2. Warmup: (5 Minutes) Copy the first two lines exactly as shown; then throw the carriage twice and type the sentence 10 times.

```
fr4 fr4 fr4 f$f f$f f$f ju7 ju7 ju7 j&j j&j j&j
f$f j&j f$f j&j f$f j&j f$f j&j f$f j&j f$f j&j

Fox & Co. offers De Luxe Refrigerators at $172.50.
```

## 3. Skill-Building Work: (20 Minutes)
(a) Preview Practice on Words and Phrases............ 3 minutes
(b) Two 1-Minute Timings and Word Practice............ 3 minutes
(c) Two 5-Minute Timings and Word Practice............14 minutes
_____
20 minutes

First:  **Preview Practice.** Each word and phrase 3 times.

```
others...typing...awkward...quickly...slowing
possible...increase...practice...smoothly...
familiar...trouble...difficult...particular...
it is...at the...you can...and the...have been
that are...with the...you will...for you
```

**Second: Machine Adjustments for Timed Typing.**
      (a) Clear all tab stops.
      (b) Set a tab stop 5 spaces from left margin.
      (c) Set line space gauge for **double** spacing.


**Third:    Two 1-Minute Timings.**


```
                                  5
      It is not possible to type all words at the same
10                          15                          20
speed.   Some words are easy to type; others are very
                    24
awkward to finger.
```


**Fourth: Two 5-Minute Timings.**


```
                                  5
      It is not possible to type all words at the same
10                          15                          20
speed.   Some words are easy to type; others are very

awkward to finger.
            25                              30
      You can increase your typing speed and accuracy
          35                              40
by typing the awkward words slowly and the easy ones
          45                              50
quickly.   Practice the words which give you trouble.
      55                          60
Practice both the easy and difficult words until you
      65                          70
can type them smoothly and accurately.
                    75                              80
      After a while, you will be familiar with the
                    85                              90
words that have been slowing you down, and at the
                    95                              100
same time you will know which words you can type
                        105
fast.   Soon you will type all words more smoothly
110           113
and accurately.
```

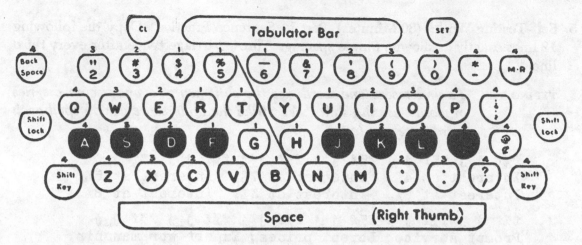

**4. New Key Control:** (10 Minutes)  Learning to use % and _ (Underscore).

% is controlled by the **F** finger.  Use right shift key.
_ is controlled by the **J** finger.  Use left shift key.

### Step 1—New Key Preview

Using the shift key, reach and touch the center of each new key; then return fingers quickly to home base.  Practice it this way—Shift, Reach, Return . . . until you can do it smoothly.  Think of the finger and the new key it controls.

### Step 2—New Key Tryout

To underscore, first type the word; then backspace to the first letter, and strike the underscore for each letter.

```
f%f  f%f  f%f  f%f  f%f  f%f   j_j  j_j  j_j  j_j  j_j  j_j
f%f  j_j  f%f  j_j  f%f  j_j   f%f  j_j  f%f  j_j  f%f  j_j
```

Deduct 5%.  Deduct 5%.  Deduct 5%.  Deduct 5%.
Do it <u>now</u>.  Do it <u>now</u>.  Do it <u>now</u>.  Do it <u>now</u>.

5. **Self-Testing Work:** (30 Minutes) Part 1. Sentence Practice. Copy the following 12 lines exactly as shown. Single spacing. Throw carriage twice after every third line.

TYPING TIP: *To underscore one word, use the shift key. To underscore a series of words, use the shift lock. Strike the underscore as you spell each word letter by letter.*

```
f%f j_j f%f j_j f%f j_j f%f j_j f%f j_j f%f j_j
Interest at 4%.  Interest at 7%.  Interest at 5%.
Interest at 6%.  Interest at 3%.  Interest at 8%.

f%f j_j f%f j_j f%f j_j f%f j_j f%f j_j f%f j_j
Prompt service; Lowest prices; Expert workmanship.
Underscore for emphasis.  Underscore for emphasis.

f%f j_j f%f j_j f%f j_j f%f j_j f%f j_j f%f j_j
City of New Orleans offers 2 1/4% and 2 1/2% bonds.
City of Los Angeles offers 2 3/8% and 2 1/4% bonds.

f%f j_j f%f j_j f%f j_j f%f j_j f%f j_j f%f j_j
Save from 12% to 18% on Superb Quality Jackets.
Save from 10% to 15% on Superb Quality Blouses.
```

*In figures, do not space before or after the comma.*
*Do not space before or after the decimal point.*

Part 2. Paragraph Practice. **Double** spacing. Copy each paragraph **once**.

```
Since our terms are 2% 10 days, 30 days net, Cox

& Vinson are not entitled to the discount of $14.90

which they have deducted from our invoice of November

27, 1953.

James inherited $1,450 from his father.  This sum

he invested in United States Savings Bonds which yield

approximately 3% interest.  These bonds are an excel-

lent investment--the safest in the world.

You may deduct a discount of 3% from the prices

quoted on Eureka Skates shown on page 75 of our 1956

catalog.  If payment is made within 10 days after date

of invoice, you may deduct an extra 1% discount.
```

6. **Corrective Work:** (5 Minutes) As usual.

**7. Challenge Work:** (5 Minutes) Here is another challenge to your ability to type a perfect paragraph:

```
           Lenox & Smith advertise Oriental Rugs in the
     following quantities and sizes:  50 Lillehans, size
     9 x 15 at $290 less 5%; 25 Persian Sarouks, size
     8 x 12 at $275 less 6%; 18 Kutajah Rugs, size 12 x 14
     at $260 less 3%.  All sales for cash only.
```

# LESSON 25

**Aim:** (a) To develop sustained typing skill by 5-Minute Timings.
(b) To learn to use # (Number Sign) and ' (Apostrophe).

1. **Machine Adjustments:**
    (a) Paper Guide:  At 0.
    (b) Line Space Gauge:  For Single Spacing.
    (c) Margin Stops:  For **Pica** type..................................at 15 and 70.
        For **Elite** type.........................at 25 and 80.
    (d) Top Margin:  10 lines from top edge of paper.

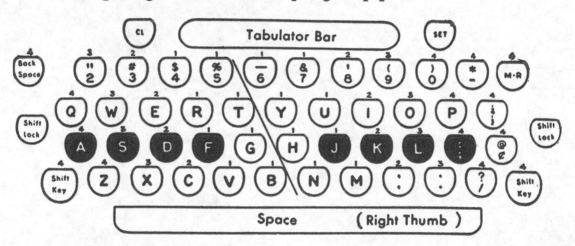

2. **Warmup:** (5 Minutes)  Copy the first two lines exactly as shown; then throw the carriage twice and type the sentence 10 times.

```
frf f4f f$f juj j7j j&j ftf f5f f%f jyj j6j j_j
frf f4f f$f juj j7j j&j ftf f5f f%f jyj j6j j_j
```

```
Zale & De Veaux offer Blue Serge at $5.70 less 3%.
```

3. **Skill-Building Work:** (20 Minutes)
    (a) Preview Practice on Words and Phrases................. 3 minutes
    (b) Two 1-Minute Timings and Word Practice............... 3 minutes
    (c) Two 5-Minute Timings and Word Practice................14 minutes
                                                            ────
                                                            20 minutes

    First:     Preview Practice.  Each word and phrase 3 times.

```
strike...lightly...learned...general...material
centered...necessary...centering...difficult...
sometimes...backspacer...appearance...attractive
impressions...horizontally...in the...to be...
with the...will be...has been
```

120

Second: **Machine Adjustments for Timed Typing.**
   (a) Clear all tab stops.
   (b) Set a tab stop 5 spaces from left margin.
   (c) Set line space gauge for **double** spacing.

Third: **Two 1-Minute Timings.**

<pre>
                         5
     To avoid light and dark impressions on the page,
10                  15                          20
strike every key with the same force.  If you strike
                    25                          30
every key with the same force, every letter will be
               34
of the same shade.
</pre>

Fourth: **Two 5-Minute Timings.**

<pre>
                          5
     To avoid light and dark impressions on the page,
10                  15                          20
strike every key with the same force.  If you strike
                    25                          30
every key with the same force, every letter will be
               35                          40
of the same shade and the general appearance of your
                45
work will be attractive.
                    50
     Sometimes, of course, it may be necessary to
  55                       60
darken a letter that has been struck very lightly
  65                       70
and is difficult to read.  In such case, use the
  75                       80
backspacer and strike the letter again lightly.
          85                          90
     The backspacer is used also for centering
               95                          100
horizontally.  As you have learned, you set the
                    105                         110
carriage at the center of the page and backspace
                    115                         120
once for every two strokes in the material to be
      121
centered.
</pre>

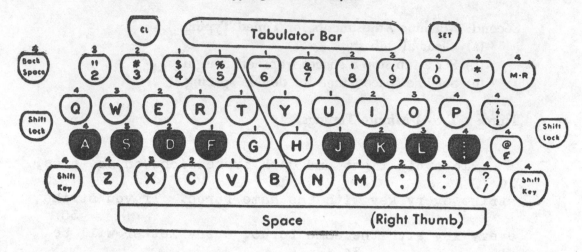

**4. New Key Control:** (10 Minutes) Learning to use # and ' keys.
# is controlled by the **D** finger. Use right shift key.
' is controlled by the **K** finger. Use left shift key.

## Step 1—New Key Preview

Using the shift key, reach and touch the center of each new key; then return fingers quickly to home base. Follow these steps—Shift, Reach, Return . . . until you can do it smoothly. Think of the finger and the key it controls.

## Step 2—New Key Tryout

```
d#d d#d d#d d#d d#d d#d k'k k'k k'k k'k k'k k'k
d#d k'k d#d k'k d#d k'k d#d k'k d#d k'k d#d k'k

#3 points; #3 points; #3 points; #3 points; #3 points;
8 o'clock; 8 o'clock; 8 o'clock; 8 o'clock; 8 o'clock;
```

5. **Self-Testing Work:** (30 Minutes) Part 1. Sentence Practice. Copy the following 12 lines exactly as shown. Single spacing.

*The symbol # means **number** when it is typed before the figure.*
*The symbol # means **pounds** when it is typed after the figure.*
*For exclamation mark: type period, backspace, and type apostrophe.*

```
d#d k'k d#d k'k d#d k'k d#d k'k d#d k'k d#d k'k
Track #3; Track #8; Track #2; Track #9; Track #7;
Order #4; Order #6; Order #5; Order #1; Order #3;

d#d k'k d#d k'k d#d k'k d#d k'k d#d k'k d#d k'k
2# beans; 9# sugar; 3# coffee; 8# butter; 4# liver;
4# sugar; 5# beans; 7# butter; 5# coffee; 6# steak;

d#d k'k d#d k'k d#d k'k d#d k'k d#d k'k d#d k'k
Car #72198 left the yard at 7 o'clock this morning.
Car #40563 left the yard at 9 o'clock this morning.

d#d k'k d#d k'k d#d k'k d#d k'k d#d k'k d#d k'k
Use the period and apostrophe for exclamation mark!
Use the period and apostrophe for exclamation mark!
```

Part 2. Paragraph Practice. **Double** spacing. Copy each paragraph once.

```
     To make an exclamation mark, type an apostrophe,
backspace, and type a period lightly.  Space twice
after an exclamation mark at the end of a sentence,
as you do after a period and after a question mark.

     The exclamation mark is used after words,
phrases, or sentences to indicate surprise or strong
emotion.  Examples: It's truly amazing!  It's a lie!
These pens are guaranteed for 10 years!

     Meet me at my office--room 295--at 9 o'clock,
Thursday, February 27.  Mr. Zims of Dixson & O'Brien
will be here to discuss their contract for construct-
ing the warehouse.

     Case #9120 containing 65 dozen #27 Black Arrow
Socks at $2.75 and weighing 250# was shipped from the
factory at 10 o'clock on Friday, January 19.
```

6. **Corrective Work:** (5 Minutes) As usual.

**7. Challenge Work:** (5 Minutes)  Aim for a perfect copy of the following paragraph —on your first try!

The shipment of #6 Glass Jars weighing 325# was forwarded on September 14 in D. L. & W. Car #917653. Another shipment of #8 size jars, estimated to weigh 350#, is now being loaded in P. R. R. Car #63195 and should reach you this week.

# LESSON 26

**Aim:** (a) To develop sustained typing skill by 5-Minute Timings.

(b) To learn to use the ( ) (Parentheses).

## 1. Machine Adjustments:

(a) Paper Guide: At 0.

(b) Line Space Gauge: For Single Spacing.

(c) Margin Stops:  For **Pica** type........................at 15 and 70.

For **Elite** type........................at 25 and 80.

(d) Top Margin: 10 lines from top edge of paper.

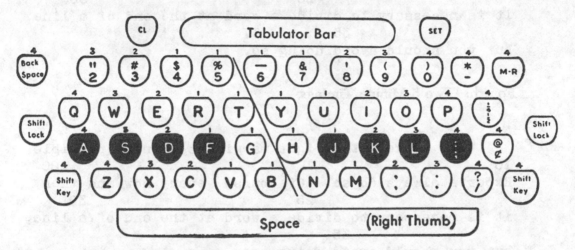

## 2. Warmup: (5 Minutes) Copy the first two lines exactly as shown; then throw the carriage twice and type the sentence 10 times:

```
f4f f$f j7j j&j f5f f%f j6j j_j d3d d#d k8k k'k
d3d d#d k8k k'k f4f f$f j7j j&j f5f f%f j6j j_j

Cox Service Company's bonds, Serial #59, yield 6%.
```

## 3. Skill-Building Work: (20 Minutes)

(a) Preview Practice on Words and Phrases................. 3 minutes

(b) Two 1-Minute Timings and Word Practice.............. 3 minutes

(c) Two 5-Minute Timings and Word Practice...............14 minutes
                                                    ‾‾‾‾‾‾‾‾‾‾
                                                    20 minutes

First:      **Preview Practice.** Each word and phrase 3 times:

```
margin...divide...always...experts...warning...
possible...carriage...division...syllable...
separate...necessary...pronounced...at the...
to the...for the...you will...do not...from the
```

125

**Second: Machine Adjustments for Timed Typing.**
  (a) Clear all tab stops.
  (b) Set a tab stop 5 spaces from left margin.
  (c) Set line space gauge for **double** spacing.

**Third:  Two 1-Minute Timings.**

```
                          5
      Try to keep the right margin as even as possible.
10                      15                          20
Experts always do so.  Of course, every now and then,
                      25                          30
it is necessary to divide a word at the end of a line,
              35        37
but you should avoid doing so.
```

**Fourth:  Two 5-Minute Timings.**

```
                            5
      Try to keep the right margin as even as possible.
10                      15                          20
Experts always do so.  Of course, every now and then,
                      25                          30
it is necessary to divide a word at the end of a line,
              35
but you should avoid doing so.
                  40                          45
      Listen for the warning bell.  When it rings,
                  50                          55
finish the word and throw the carriage for the next
              60                          65
line.  Thus, you will not have to divide many words.
              70                          75
Here are a few simple rules for word division:
                  80
      First, divide only after a full syllable.
  85                          90
Second, do not divide a word that is pronounced as
      95                          100
one syllable, such as, though, shipped, bought.
          105                          110
Third, do not separate one letter from the rest of
      114
a word.
```

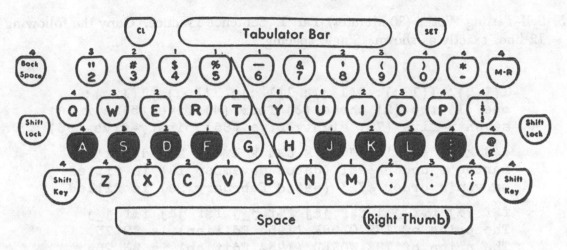

**4. New Key Control:** (10 Minutes) Learning to use ( ) (Parentheses).
Left parenthesis ( is controlled by the **L** finger.   Use left shift key.
Right parenthesis ) is controlled by the  **;**  finger.    Use left shift key.

### Step 1—New Key Preview

Using the left shift key, reach and touch the center of each new key; then return fingers quickly to home base.  Finger each new key as you say it to yourself—to memorize its location.

### Step 2—New Key Tryout

*Keep elbows close to body.*

```
l(l l(l l(l l(l l(l l(l  ;); ;); ;); ;); ;); ;);
l(l ;); l(l ;); l(l ;); l(l ;); l(l ;); l(l ;);

pump (#10); pump (#10); pump (#10); pump (#10);
jack (#10); jack (#10); jack (#10); jack (#10);
```

5. **Self-Testing Work:** (30 Minutes)  Part 1.  Sentence Practice.  Copy the following
12 lines exactly as shown.  Single spacing.

```
1(1 ;); 1(1 ;); 1(1 ;); 1(1 ;); 1(1 ;); 1(1 ;);
one (1) two (2) three (3) four (4) five (5) six (6)
seventy-five (75) eighty-five (85) ninety-five (95)

d#d k'k d#d k'k d#d k'k d#d k'k d#d k'k d#d k'k
Barton's order #981 (dated November 19) is filled.
Marvin's order #723 (dated February 26) is filled.

f$f j&j f%f j_j f$f j&j f%f j_j f$f j&j f%f j_j
The price of THE GLOBE (1953 Edition) is $2.75.
The price of THE WORLD (1954 Edition) is $3.25.

1(1 ;); 1(1 ;); 1(1 ;); 1(1 ;); 1(1 ;); 1(1 ;);
Train No. 82034 (New York Central) left at 3:24 a.m.
Train No. 17965 (New York Central) left at 8:05 p.m.
```

**Part 2.**  Paragraph Practice.  **Double** spacing.  Copy each paragraph **once**.

```
        The contract specified (a) 12 boxes to a carton;
(b) cartons fastened by wire bands; (c) each carton
plainly identified; (d) complete delivery by May 1957.
        Don't miss MY LITTLE MARGIE (TV'S favorite)
tonight at 8:30 on Station WXLT TV Channel #5.  Pre-
sented by Scott & Manville Paper Company.
        The Pierce Car Company (reorganized) is now dis-
playing its new 2-passenger car at nine hundred and
fifty dollars ($950).  It will go 18 miles (average)
on one gallon of gasoline.
        To be placed on the free mailing list, please
(1) use school stationery; (2) indicate the business
courses you are teaching; (3) mail your request to
our nearest office.
```

6. **Corrective Work:** (5 Minutes)  As usual.

**7. Challenge Work:** (5 Minutes) Try for a perfect copy of the following paragraph
—on your first attempt.

        We understand that the traditional colors in
your school are Royal Blue (for the girls) and Orange
(for the boys).  We shall be glad to furnish the caps
and gowns (made of Lido Cloth) in the colors desired
at $8.75 per outfit.

# LESSON 27

**Aim:** (a) To develop sustained typing skill by 5-Minute Timings.
(b) To learn to use " (Quotation Marks) and * (Asterisk).

**1. Machine Adjustments:**
   (a) Paper Guide:  At 0.
   (b) Line Space Gauge:  For Single Spacing.
   (c) Margin Stops:  For **Pica** type......................at 15 and 70.
            For **Elite** type......................at 25 and 80.
   (d) Top Margin:  10 lines from top edge of paper.

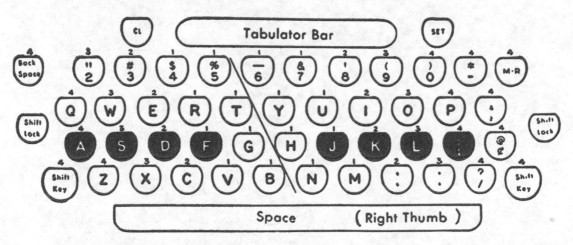

**2. Warmup:** (5 Minutes) Copy the first two lines exactly as shown; then throw the carriage twice and type the sentence 10 times.

```
f$f j&j f%f j_j d#d k'k l(l ;); d#d k'k l(l ;);
f$f j&j f%f j_j d#d k'k l(l ;); d#d k'k l(l ;);
```

```
The banker's home was sold (at a loss) for $9,760.
```

**3. Skill-Building Work:** (20 Minutes)
   (a) Preview Practice on Words and Phrases........................ 3 minutes
   (b) Two 1-Minute Timings and Word Practice.................. 3 minutes
   (c) Two 5-Minute Timings and Word Practice.............. 14 minutes
   ————————
   20 minutes

First:    **Preview Practice.** Each word and phrase 3 times:

```
barely...faster...machine...posture...forward...
loosely...position...directly...slightly...
touching...parallel...keyboard...important...
of the...at the...in the...to the...to it
```

130

Second: Machine Adjustments for Timed Typing.
    (a) Clear all tab stops.
    (b) Set a tab stop 5 spaces from left margin.
    (c) Set line space gauge for **double** spacing.

Third:   Two 1-Minute Timings.

               5
    Your position at the machine is more important
10            15
than you think.  Good posture will help you to build
20         25
your skill at a faster rate.

Fourth:  Two 5-Minute Timings.

               5
    Your position at the machine is more important
10            15
than you think.  Good posture will help you to build
20         25
your skill at a faster rate.
              30
    Use these simple rules of good posture:  Sit
35            40
directly in front of the machine, hips well back in
45            50
the chair, body erect but leaning slightly forward.
55         60           65
Let your arms hang loosely at the sides close to the
body.
              70
    Keep all fingers curved like claws and just
75         80         85
barely touching the guide keys.  See to it that your
              90          95
hands are parallel and sloping in the same direction
             100         105
as the keyboard.  Hold your wrists low but not touching
      109
the machine.

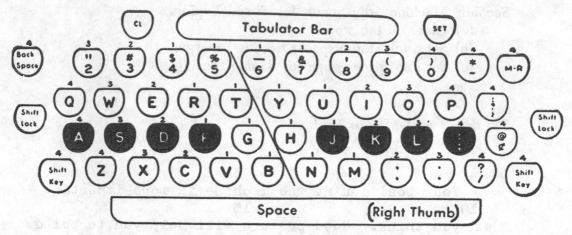

**4. New Key Control:** (10 Minutes) Learning to use " and *.
   " is controlled by the S finger.  Use right shift key.
   * is controlled by the ; finger.  Use left shift key.

### Step 1—New Key Preview

Using the shift key, reach and touch the center of each new key; then return
fingers quickly to home base.  Finger each new key several times as you say it
to yourself—to memorize its location.

### Step 2—New Key Tryout

```
s"s s"s s"s s"s s"s s"s ;*; ;*; ;*; ;*; ;*; ;*;
s"s ;*; s"s ;*; s"s ;*; s"s ;*; s"s ;*; s"s ;*;

"East"; "East"; "East"; "East"; "East"; "East";
"West"; "West"; "West"; "West"; "West"; "West";
```

**5. Self-Testing Work:** (30 Minutes) Part 1.  Sentence Practice.  Copy the following
12 lines exactly as shown.  Single spacing.

```
s"s ;*; s"s s"s ;*; s"s;*; s"s ;*; s"s ;*;
10" (10 inches); 29" (29 inches); 38" (38 inches);
12" (12 inches); 19" (19 inches); 42" (42 inches);

f$f j&j f%f j_j f$f j&j f%f j_j f$f j&j f%f j_j
19" Zenith TV Sets $137.  21" Zenith TV Sets $141.
19" Philco TV Sets $138.  21" Philco TV Sets $143.

s"s ;*; s"s ;*; s"s ;*; s"s ;*; s"s ;*; ;*;
Use the asterisk (*) for a footnote reference.
Use the asterisk (*) for a footnote reference.

s"s ;*; s"s ;*; s"s ;*; s"s ;*; s"s ;*; s"s ;*;
The steamship "Parthia" (English) arrived on June 10.
The steamship "Colombo" (Italian) arrived on July 29.
```

Part 2.  Paragraph Practice.  **Double** spacing.  Copy each paragraph **once.**

In this morning's "New York Times," Associated Market advertises #5 cans of peaches (California type) at 19¢ each.  This is 3¢ a can less than the lowest price ever quoted before on this quality.

Baxter & Company will conduct their sale of Women's "All-Wool" Blue Serge Suits (English make)* at 9 a.m. Monday, January 19.  All sizes.  Alterations free!

To celebrate its 35th anniversary, Vim offers Welbilt 36" Gas Ranges for only $69.50 and "Maytag" Automatic Washers for only $150.95.

The expression "Don't give up the ship" really means:  "Don't quit.  You can make good."  Those who succeed are ordinary folks who have a "will to win."

6. **Corrective Work:** (5 Minutes)  As usual.

7. **Challenge Work:** (5 Minutes)  Here's another challenge to you!  **A perfect copy** of the following paragraph:

Bridget was applying for the position of maid in a household where the mistress was very particular.

"Have you any references?" asked the mistress.

"Oh, yes, ma'am, lots of them," replied Bridget.

"Then why didn't you bring them with you?"

"Well," the maid explained, "to tell the truth, they're like my photographs--none of 'em do me justice."

# LESSON 28

**Aim:** (a) To develop sustained typing skill by 5-Minute Timings.
(b) To learn to use @ (At) and ¼ (One-quarter) keys.

**1. Machine Adjustments:**
    (a) Paper Guide: At 0.
    (b) Line Space Gauge: For 'Single Spacing.
    (c) Margin Stops: For Pica type.....................................at 15 and 70.
                      For Elite type........................at 25 and 80.
    (d) Top Margin: 10 lines from top edge of paper.

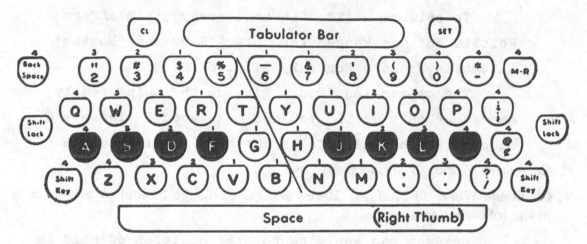

**2. Warmup:** (5 Minutes) Copy the first two lines exactly as shown; then throw the carriage twice and type the sentence 10 times.

```
f$f j&j f%f j_j d#d k'k l(l ;); ;*; s"s l(l ;); ;*;
d#d k'k f$f j&j f%f j_j s"s l(l ;); ;*; l(l ;); ;*;

"Don't give up the ship" means "Don't be a quitter."
```

**3. Skill-Building Work:** (20 Minutes)
    (a) Preview Practice on Words and Phrases.................. 3 minutes
    (b) Two 1-Minute Timings and Word Practice.............. 3 minutes
    (c) Two 5-Minute Timings and Word Practice.............14 minutes
                                                         20 minutes

**First:** **Preview Practice.** Each word and phrase 3 times:

```
thought...through...without...success...However
getting...usually...decided...hastily...definite
decision...objective...education...to do...it is
you are...you would...may be...they are
```

134

Second: Machine Adjustments for Timed Typing.
    (a) Clear all tab stops.
    (b) Set a tab stop 5 spaces from left margin.
    (c) Set line space gauge for **double** spacing.

Third:   Two 1-Minute Timings.

```
                           5
        Have you given any thought to what you want to do
10                             15                          20
when you leave school?  Most boys and girls go through
                         25                          30
school without having a clear and definite objective
           33
before them.
```

Fourth: Two 5-Minute Timings.

```
                           5
        Have you given any thought to what you want to do
10                             15                          20
when you leave school?  Most boys and girls go through
                         25                          30
school without having a clear and definite objective
                         35                          40
before them.   The result is that they are not the
                   45
success they might have been.
                   50                          55
        You may be unable to make up your mind about the
                   60                          65
kind of work you would like to do; it is not usually
              70                          75
easy to reach a decision.  And, indeed, it is not a
              80                          85
matter that should be decided upon hastily.
                        90
        However, you should, while you are getting an
   95                          100           103
education, begin to think about your career.
```

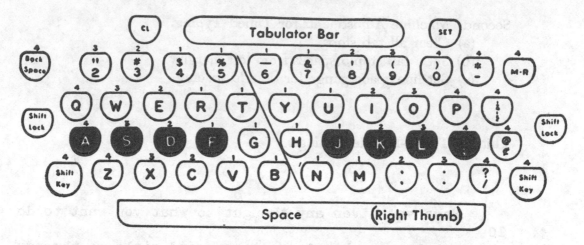

4. **New Key Control:** (10 Minutes)  Learning to use @ and ¼.
   @ is controlled by the **semicolon** finger. Use left shift key.
   ¼ is controlled by the **semicolon** finger. Use left shift key.

### Step 1—New Key Preview

Using the left shift key, reach and touch the center of each new key; then return fingers quickly to home base.  Finger each new key several times as you say it to yourself.

### Step 2—New Key Tryout

*Keep elbows close to body.  Strike keys sharply.*

;@; ;@; ;@; ;@; ;@; ;@; ;¼; ;¼; ;¼; ;¼; ;¼; ;¼;
;@; ;¼; ;@; ;¼; ;@; ;¼; ;@; ;¼; ;@; ;¼; ;@; ;¼;

5 @ 6¼¢; 5 @ 6¼¢; 5 @ 6¼¢; 5 @ 6¼¢; 5 @ 6¼¢;
4 @ 7¼¢; 4 @ 7¼¢; 4 @ 7¼¢; 4 @ 7¼¢; 4 @ 7¼¢;

**5. Self-Testing Work:** (30 Minutes) Part 1. Sentence Practice. Copy the following 12 lines exactly as shown. Single spacing.

```
12 boxes @ 10¼¢; 36 pairs @ 49¼¢; 15 dozen @ 59¼¢;
70 dozen @ 68¼¢; 50 boxes @ 74¼¢; 65 pairs @ 75¼¢;

Use the symbol / for fractions such as, 1/8, 2/3, 3/7.
Use the symbol / for fractions such as, 5/6, 7/9, 4/5.

Be consistent in typing fractions; as, ½, ¼, 1/2, 1/4.
Be consistent in typing fractions; as, ½, ¼, 1/2, 1/4.

Use the symbol # to indicate numbers; as, #39, #75.
Use the symbol $ to indicate dollars; as, $21, $80.

Have you received our order #78?  It amounts to $175.
Have you received our order #91?  It amounts to $246.

The symbols % and & are used in orders and invoices.
The symbols " and ' are used in orders and invoices.
```

Part 2. Paragraph Practice. **Double** spacing. Copy each paragraph **once**.

```
        The only fractions on your keyboard are ½ and ¼.
To make all other fractions, use the slant.  Here are
a few more examples:  3/4, 3/5, 1/10.  Such fractions
are "made" fractions.  Do not space before or after
the slant.

        When typing whole numbers and "made" fractions,
space once between the whole number and the "made"
fraction.  Note carefully the following examples:
3 2/5, 4 7/8, 2 3/4, 6 1/9.

        However, when typing whole numbers with ½ or ¼,
do not space after the whole number.  Type the whole
number and the fraction as shown in the following
examples:

        Municipal Bonds yield from 2½% to 3¼% interest.
        The distance to the lake was exactly 1¼ miles.
```

**6. Corrective Work:** (5 Minutes) As usual.

**7. Challenge Work:** (5 Minutes) Try for a perfect copy of the following paragraph:

Find the cost of the following:  156 lbs. Butter @ 71 3/4¢; 145 doz. Eggs @ 63¼¢; 170 boxes Oranges @ $5.67½¢; 350 cans California Canned Peaches @ 12¼¢; 150 lbs. Bosc Pears @ 8½¢; 125 cans (#1) Campbell's Soup @ 9¼¢; 165 lbs. Domino Granulated Sugar @ 7¼¢.

# LESSON 29

**Aim:** (a) To develop sustained typing skill by 5-Minute Timings.
      (b) To learn to type **Personal Letters—Block form.**

## 1. Machine Adjustments:
    (a) Paper Guide:  At 0.
    (b) Line Space Gauge:  For Single Spacing.
    (c) Margin Stops:  For **Pica** type......................at 15 and 70.
                   For **Elite** type.......................at 25 and 80.
    (d) Top Margin:  10 lines from top edge of paper.

## 2. Warmup: (5 Minutes)  Copy the first two lines exactly as shown; then throw the carriage twice and type the sentence 10 times.

```
f$f j&j f%f j_j d#d k'k s"s 1(1 ;); ;*; s"s ;*;
f$f j&j f%f j_j d#d k'k s"s 1(1 ;); ;*; s"s ;*;
```

```
See our #3 catalog (page 30) for Boys' "Glider" skates.
```

## 3. Skill-Building Work:  (20 Minutes)
    (a) Preview Practice on Words and Phrases................... 3 minutes
    (b) Two 1-Minute Timings and Word Practice................ 3 minutes
    (c) Two 5-Minute Timings and Word Practice..............14 minutes
                                                     ——
                                                  20 minutes

**First:**    **Preview Practice.**  Each word and phrase 3 times:

```
letter...simpler...picture...personal...business
otherwise...important...carefully...difference
attractive...impression...accurately...on the
for you...you can...to make...there is
```

**Second: Machine Adjustments for Timed Typing.**
    (a) Clear all tab stops.
    (b) Set a tab stop 5 spaces from left margin.
    (c) Set line space gauge for **double spacing.**

**Third:**    **Two 1-Minute Timings.**
```
                              5
     Letters are of two types--personal and business.
10                      15                          20
Personal letters are simpler than business letters,
                  25              28
but otherwise, there is little difference.
```
139

Fourth: Two 5-Minute Timings.

```
                                 5
            Letters are of two types--personal and business.
    10                          15                             20
    Personal letters are simpler than business letters,
                               25
    but otherwise, there is little difference.
                   30                       35
            Every letter you type should look attractive.
                   40                       45
    The way your letter looks is as important as what
                       50                       55
    it says.  Your letter speaks for you; so it should,
                   60                       65
    first of all, make a good impression.
                               70
            Try to keep your right margin as even as you
           75                       80
    can.  That makes your letter look neat and carefully
       85                       90
    done.  Type accurately.  Center your letter on the
       95                           100                    104
    paper so that it looks like a picture in a frame.
```

4. **New Work:** (15 Minutes)  Typing a Personal Letter—Block Form.
   (a) Clear tab stop set for the 5-Minute Timing.
   (b) Set a new tab stop at the center—42 (Pica); 50 (Elite).
   (c) Set line space gauge for **single** spacing.  Margin Stops as before.
   (d) Insert a full sheet; space up 16 times from top edge.
   (e) Type address, date, and closing at the center.  Jump the carriage to that
       point—press the tab bar or tab key.
   (f) Type the greeting—Dear Tom—six lines below the date.

(See Model, Page 141)

                              750 Western Boulevard   Address on
                              Chicago 6, Illinois     line 16
                              January 14, 19--        from
                                                      top edge.
                                                      Start at
                                                      center.

On
line 6      Dear Tom:
below
date.       You can learn touch typing--by yourself.

            TYPING MADE SIMPLE--the latest book for beginners--shows
            you how.  This book tells you in simple, man-to-man talk
            exactly what to do, how to do it, and how to keep score
            of your progress.

Space       I've just finished the whole course--35 lessons.  And
twice       I'm convinced that touch typing is easier than you think.
between
paragraphs  What do you think of this letter--by a beginner?  My
            average speed is 18 words a minute.  If I can put in
            about an hour of practice every day, I think I can soon
            boost it to 30.

            Let me know how you're doing in your new job.

                              Sincerely yours,        Closing
                                                       at center.


PERSONAL LETTER—BLOCK FORM

5. **Self-Testing Work:** (30 Minutes) Retype the letter to Tom. This time aim for a **perfect** copy. Then insert a fresh sheet and type the letter below—to test your skill.

REMINDER:    Address on line 16 from top edge—at center.
Greeting—Dear Alice—on line 6 below date.
Space twice between paragraphs.
Closing—Sincerely—at center.

```
                              149 Garfield Lane
                              Bangor, Maine
                              June 17, 1957

        Dear Alice:

        We were thrilled to hear that you won a prize in the
        school essay contest.

        Congratulations on your success!  We hope that you will
        have many more such happy accomplishments.

        It's quite a while since you last visited us, and we're
        so eager to have you with us again for a few days.  You
        would never recognize our shack.  Dad and Gerald have
        built an extension to the porch and have repainted the
        whole place.

        Please write me if you can spend the first week in July
        with us so we can plan some fun together.

                              Sincerely,
```

6. **Number Review:** (5 Minutes) The following 10 lines stress the figures 1, 4, 5, 6, and 7. Test your mastery of these figures. Try for a perfect copy.

```
        fr4f ju7j ft5f jy6j fr4f ju7j ft5f jy6j fr4f ju7j
        for4 gnu7 bit5 dry6 nor6 flu7 hit5 try6 nor4 gnu7

        nor 4 gnu 7 bit 5 sly 6 for 4 gnu 7 sit 5 fly 6
        mar 4 flu 7 kit 5 dry 6 war 4 flu 7 hit 5 sly 6

        11 men; 74 women; 14 boys; 47 girls; Total 146
        47 men; 14 women; 74 boys; 11 girls; Total 146

        5 and 7 and 4 and 6 and 1 and 41 and 65 and 175
        7 and 5 and 6 and 4 and 7 and 14 and 56 and 715

        4 and 7 and 5 and 6 and 1 and 14 and 56 and 517
        1 and 6 and 4 and 7 and 5 and 41 and 65 and 175
```

# LESSON 30

**Aim:** (a) To develop sustained typing skill by 5-Minute Timings.
     (b) To learn to type **business letters—block form.**
(For detailed information see *Business Letter Writing Made Simple*).

## 1. Machine Adjustments:
    (a) Paper Guide:  At 0.
    (b) Line Space Gauge:  For Single Spacing.
    (c) Margin Stops:  For Pica type........................at 15 and 70.
                   For Elite type........................at 25 and 80.
    (d) Top Margin:  10 lines from top edge of paper.

## 2. Warmup: (5 Minutes)
Copy the first two lines exactly as shown; then throw the carriage twice and type the sentence 10 times:

```
f4f  j7j  f5f  j6j  d3d  k8k  s2s  l9l  ;0;  ;/;  ;¢;  ;½;  ;-;
f4f  j7j  f5f  j6j  d3d  k8k  s2s  l9l  ;0;  ;/;  ;¢;  ;½;  ;-;
```

```
The sum of 10 and 29 and 38 and 47 and 56 and 7 is 187.
```

## 3 Skill-Building Work: (20 Minutes)
    (a) Preview Practice on Words and Phrases.............. 3 minutes
    (b) Two 1-Minute Timings and Word Practice.............. 3 minutes
    (c) Two 5-Minute Timings and Word Practice...............14 minutes
                                                    20 minutes

**First:**   **Preview Practice.** Each word and phrase 3 times:

```
typing...letter...writing...company...address
printed...business...consists...outgoing...
wrinkled...therefore...letterhead...appearance...
attractive...responsible...correspondence...
in the...of the...and the...from the...that is
```

**Second: Machine Adjustments for Timed Typing.**
    (a) Clear all tab stops.
    (b) Set a tab stop 5 spaces from left margin.
    (c) Set line space gauge for **double** spacing.

**Third:**   **Two 1-Minute Timings.**

```
                              5                              10
    In the business world, much of the typing consists
                        15                              20
of letter writing.  Outgoing business letters are typed
            25
on letterhead paper.
```

143

Fourth:  Two 5-Minute Timings.

                                      5                                        10
In the business world, much of the typing consists
                        15                                  20
of letter writing.  Outgoing business letters are typed
                  25                                  30
on letterhead paper; that is, paper on which the company
              35
name and address are printed.
                40                                  45
The letterhead paper used for business correspond-
            50                                  55
ence is 8½ inches wide and 11 inches long.  Plain paper
        60
is used for carbon copies.
          65                                  70
The typist is responsible for the appearance of
      75                                  80
the letter.  The good typist, therefore, takes pains
    85                                  90                                  95
to make every letter attractive.  The print should be
                100                                 105
dark and even, and the type should be clean.  The paper
            110                                 114
should be fresh--never soiled or wrinkled.

**4. New Work Tryout:** (15 Minutes) Business Letter—Block Form.
    (a) Business letters are typed on printed letterheads usually 8½ by 11 inches. To look attractive, a letter should appear like a picture in a frame. You can turn out attractive letters by keeping these two points in mind:

        1. Left and right margins should be almost equal.  The right margin may be slightly less than the left.

        2. Top and bottom margins should be almost equal.  The bottom margin may be a little wider than the top.

    (b) Business letters are of three lengths: short, average, long.  Experience will teach you how to estimate the margins for attractive letter placement.  Meanwhile, here is an easy placement guide to get you started:

*Letters of About 100 Words*

Pica Type . . . . . . . . . . . 15-70-16-6
Elite Type . . . . . . . . . . 25-80-16-6

*Remember
these 3
placement
points.*

(1) The first two figures are the left and right margin stops—as usual.

(2) The figure 16 means that you type the date on line 16 from top edge of paper.

(3) The inside address is typed on line 6 from date.

*Letters Over 100 Words*

(1) Same margin stops.
(2) Same top margin.
(3) For every 25 words over 100, subtract 1 from 6—for spaces between date and inside address.

(c) Now, see the next page and study the model of a Block Form Business Letter. Learn the names of the parts of the letter and the spacing between the parts—both are indicated. Then insert an 8½ by 11 sheet and copy the model—step by step.

1st: Clear the tab stop set for the 5-Minute Timing.
2nd: Set a new tab stop at center of paper: 42 (Pica); 50 (Elite).
3rd: Set line space gauge for Single Spacing.

Date on
line 16
from top.
Backspace
from right
margin.

February 18, 19--

Figures in
parentheses
indicate
number of
single spaces
between each
part of letter.

(6)

Inside
Address

James Thompson Company, Inc.
267 North Second Street
Jacksonville 12, Florida

(2)

Salutation    Gentlemen:

(2)

Thank you for your letter of February 15, informing us
that the shipment of Boys' hats has not yet reached you.
We regret this delay as much as you do.

(2)

Body
of
letter

Our traffic manager has already telegraphed the railroad
company to put an immediate tracer after this shipment,
and we assure you that we shall keep after the railroad
company until the goods arrive.

(2)

If the shipment does not reach you by February 23, please
wire us at our expense, and we shall send you a duplicate
lot by express the same day.

(2)

Very truly yours          Complimentary Close

(2)

MARVIN HAT COMPANY        Firm Name      Last 4
                                         lines
                                         at
                          (4)            center.

Initials
of
dictator       LS:MB
and
typist

Lawrence Smith            Dictator
President                 Title

BLOCK FORM.   90 words.  Placement Points:  15-70-16-6 (Pica)
                                            25-80-16-6 (Elite)
Note the block inside address; block paragraph
beginnings; block complimentary closing.

5. **Self-Testing Work:** (30 Minutes) See whether you can type both the letters below. Arrange each on a separate sheet, in block form (like the model on page 146). Each letter contains about 100 words.

April 7, 19--

Bowman Paper Company
179 Elm Street
Syracuse 7, New York

Gentlemen:

We appreciate your check for $343 in payment of our invoice of March 15.

However, we are obliged to return this remittance to you because you deducted a discount of 2 percent after the discount period had elapsed. As you know, our terms are 2 percent 10 days from date of shipment, regardless of delivery date, or 30 days net.

We all want to be fair to the other fellow. If we allowed this deduction, it would be unfair to the majority of our customers who discount their bills within the allotted time.

Won't you mail us your check for the full amount.

Very truly yours
BROWN PAPER COMPANY
Martin Bradley
MB:NF    Credit Manager

June 3, 19--

Mr. James Barnett
385 Henry Street
Chicago 4, Illinois

Dear Sir:

Thank you very much for your letter of May 27 expressing your desire to open a charge account with us. We are always glad to welcome a new customer and assure you of our desire to serve you.

You are, of course, familiar with such blanks as the one attached. All responsible business firms use such forms to secure information that may facilitate the opening of a charge account.

May we, therefore, trouble you to fill out this form and return it in the inclosed stamped envelope. We shall then make the necessary inquiries to hasten the opening of your account.

Very truly yours
JAMES ROBINSON & CO.
Raymond Cole
RC:JH    Credit Manager

**6. Number Review:** (5 Minutes)  The following 10 lines stress the figures 2, 3, 8, 9, 0.
See whether you can type a **perfect** copy.

```
     de3d ki8k sw2s lo9l ;p0; de3d ki8k sw2s lo9l ;p0;
     ire3 ski8 low2 two9 lip0 ire3 ski8 tow2 two9 lip0

     3 and 8 and 2 and 9 and 0 and 9 and 8 and 3 and 2
     8 and 3 and 2 and 0 and 9 and 3 and 9 and 8 and 2

     29 and 38 and 90 and 83 and 92 and 20 and 80 and 30
     20 and 83 and 93 and 82 and 29 and 38 and 92 and 80

     Canal 2-9380; Castle 2-3928; Spring 3-2903; CA 5-2894
     Axtel 8-0293; Spring 3-0329; Castle 9-3028; SP 8-0982

     Rector 9-0932; Bryant 3-8032; Walker 8-3028; RE 2-0389
     Oregon 3-0823; Oxford 2-2030; Lehigh 3-9089; OX 8-3290
```

# LESSON 31

**Aim:** (a) To develop sustained typing skill by 5-Minute Timings.
(b) To learn to type **business letters—semiblock form.**

## 1. Machine Adjustments:
(a) Paper Guide:  At 0.
(b) Line Space Gauge:  For Single Spacing.
(c) Margin Stops:  For **Pica** type . . . . . . . . . . . . . . . . . . . . . . . . . . . at 15 and 70.
For **Elite** type . . . . . . . . . . . . . . . . . . . . . . . at 25 and 80.
(d) Top Margin:  10 lines from top edge of paper.

## 2. Warmup: (5 Minutes) Copy the first two lines exactly as shown; then throw the carriage twice and type the sentence 10 times.

```
frf juj ftf jyj fgf jhj ded kik sws lol aqa ;p;
fvf jmj fbf jnj dcd k,k sxs l.l aza ;/; ;¢; ;½;
```

We expect Vermont to yield large blocks of quartz.

## 3. Skill-Building Work: (20 Minutes)
(a) Preview Practice on Words and Phrases. . . . . . . . . . . . . . . . . 3 minutes
(b) Two 1-Minute Timings and Word Practice. . . . . . . . . . . . . . . 3 minutes
(c) Two 5-Minute Timings and Word Practice. . . . . . . . . . . . . . . 14 minutes
                                                                          ——————
                                                                          20 minutes

First:    **Preview Practice.** Each word and phrase 3 times:

device...margin...simply...holding...machine
already...extreme...desired...carriage...
tabulator...labor-saving...on the...to the...
with the...do not...you have

Second: **Machine Adjustments for Timed Typing.**
(a) Clear all tab stops.
(b) Set a tab stop 5 spaces from left margin.
(c) Set line space gauge for **double** spacing.

Third:   **Two 1-Minute Timings.**

```
                            5                                    10
    The tabulator key or bar is a labor-saving device.
                          15                          20
By holding it down, you make the carriage jump to any
                  24
point on the scale.
```

Fourth:  **Two 5-Minute Timings.**

```
                               5                                    10
       The tabulator key or bar is a labor-saving device.
                        15                      20
By holding it down, you make the carriage jump to any

point on the scale.
           25                      30
       First, of course, you have to clear the machine
       35                      40
of all tab stops that may already be set.  To do so,
       45                      50
move the left and right margin stops to the extreme
       55                      60
ends; then hold down the Clear Key and move the
       65                      70
carriage from side to side with the carriage release
       75
key.
                                  80
       To set your own tab stops, move the carriage
       85                      90
to each desired point on the scale and press the Set
       95
Key.
```

4. **New Work Tryout:** (15 Minutes) Business Letter—Semiblock Form.
    (a) Inside address is blocked at the margin.
    (b) First line of each paragraph is indented 5 spaces.
    (c) Complimentary close, firm name, dictator's name, are blocked.

Copy, step by step, the following model.
    1st:  Clear tab stop set for 5-minute timing.
    2nd:  Set one new tab stop 5 spaces from left margin; another at center
          of paper for the closing—42 (Pica); 50 (Elite).
    3rd:  Set line space gauge for Single Spacing.

(See Model, Page 151)

September 17, 19--

Date on
line 16
from top.
Backspace
from right
margin.

6 spaces
between
date and
inside
address.

2 spaces
between
inside
address
and the
salutation.

Allen Clothing Company
285 Webster Avenue
Akron 3, Ohio

Gentlemen:

Thank you for your check for $300, which has been credited to your account.

2 spaces
between
paragraphs.

It is not customary for us to grant extensions on accounts, as the terms indicated on the invoice are a definite part of our sales policy. We will make an exception in your case, however, because we believe that our delay in shipping your order must have caused you some loss of sales.

We request that you cooperate with us by paying the balance of $215 by the first of next month. It would be wise for you to close this account to maintain your credit standing with the bank.

(2)

Very truly yours
(2)
EXCLUSIVE CLOTHIERS, INC.

(4)

Figures
indicate
number of
single
spaces
between
each
part.

Martin Goldsmith
Office Manager

MG:RL

SEMIBLOCK FORM. 100 words. Placement Points: 15-70-16-6 (Pica)
25-80-16-6 (Elite)

# LESSON 33

**Aim:** (a) To develop sustained typing skill by 5-Minute Timings.

(b) To learn to type 2-Column Tabulations.

## 1. Machine Adjustments:

(a) Paper Guide:  At 0.

(b) Line Space Gauge:  For Double Spacing.

(c) Margin Stops:  For **Pica** type.........................at 15 and 70.

For **Elite** type........................at 25 and 80.

(d) Top Margin:  10 lines from top edge of paper.

## 2. Warmup: (5 Minutes) Copy the first two lines exactly as shown; then throw the carriage twice and type the sentence 10 times:

```
frf juj ded kik sws lol aqa ;p; fvf jmj fgf jhj fbf jnj
dcd k,k sxs l.l aza ;/; fgf jhj fbf jnj fvf jmj dcd k,k
```

```
The quick, old judge admired the boy for his zeal.
```

## 3. Skill-Building Work: (20 Minutes)

(a) Preview Practice on Words and Phrases.............. 3 minutes

(b) Two 1-Minute Timings and Word Practice................ 3 minutes

(c) Two 5-Minute Timings and Word Practice.............14 minutes

20 minutes

**First:**    **Preview Practice.** Each word and phrase 3 times:

```
typing...number...begins...column...between...
longest...material...vertical...subtract...fraction...
carriage...placement...remainder...backspace...
tabulation...understand...horizontal...in the...
of the...at that...on which...there is
```

**Second: Machine Adjustments for Timed Typing.**

(a) Clear all tab stops.

(b) Set a tab stop 5 spaces from left margin.

(c) Set line space gauge for **double** spacing.

**Third:**    **Two 1-Minute Timings.**

*Repeat sentence as many times as you can.*

```
                        5
    Tabulation means typing material in table form
    10                        15        17
to make it easy to read and understand.
```

159

Fourth: Two 5-Minute Timings.

                             5

     Tabulation means typing material in table form

10                    15

to make it easy to read and understand.

            20                   25

     For vertical placement, subtract the total number

        30               35

of lines from 66 and divide the remainder by 2.  The

        40           45

answer shows the line number on which the typing begins.

   50           55

If there is a fraction, ignore it.

         60                65

     For horizontal placement, count the strokes in the

       70           75

longest line in each column and add 6 spaces between

     80          85

columns.  The total shows the width of the tabulation.

    90          95

     Center the carriage; backspace half the width of

    100         105

the tabulation; set your left margin at that point.

   110         115

Tap out on the space bar the longest line in the first

   120        125

column plus 6 more between the first two columns and

   130        135

set a tab stop at that point.  Do the same for all other

   140

columns.

**4. New Work Tryout:** (15 Minutes) 2-Column Tabulation.
Tabulation means typing material in table form—to make it easy to read and understand.  Let us work out, step by step, the following tabulation job:

```
                 HIGH SCHOOL SUBJECTS

          Algebra              Home Economics
          Arithmetic           Hygiene
          Biology              Italian
          Bookkeeping          Latin

          Chemistry            Mechanical Drawing
          Commercial Law       Music
          English              Natural Science
          French               Physics

          Geometry             Spanish
          German               Social Studies
          Health Education     Trigonometry
          Hebrew               Typewriting
```

First:      **Machine Adjustments.**
          (a) Move margin stops to opposite ends.
          (b) Clear all tab stops.
          (c) Set line space gauge for **single** spacing.

Second:  Insert paper, top edge even with alignment scale.

Third:     Determine **vertical placement**—for equal top and bottom margins:
          1. Count the typewritten lines.  (13)
          2. Count the blank lines between the typewritten lines.  (3)
          3. Add: 13 plus 3 is 16.  The tabulation occupies 16 lines.
          4. Subtract 16 lines from 66—the total number of lines on a full sheet
             of standard typing paper.  16 from 66 is 50.  The 50 remaining blank
             lines are divided in half—for equal top and bottom margins.
          5. Divide 50 by 2.  Result: 25.
          6. Space 25 times from top edge of paper.
          7. Move the carriage to the center of the paper—42 (Pica); 50 (Elite).
          8. Center and type the heading—HIGH SCHOOL SUBJECTS.  Then
             space down twice for the next step—horizontal placement.

Fourth: Determine **horizontal placement**—for equal left and right margins:
1. For each column in the tabulation, draw a horizontal line:

_____    _____

2. Write on the lines the number of letters and spaces in the longest line in each column:

        16 _____           18 _____

3. Between the lines, write the number of spaces to leave between the columns.  Six spaces are equal to about a half inch—an easy eye span in reading; so let us leave 6 spaces:

        16 _____ 6 _____ 18

4. Add the figures in step 3: 16 plus 6 plus 18 equals 40.
   The tabulation is 40 horizontal spaces.
5. Move carriage to center of paper:  42 (Pica); 50 (Elite).
6. Backspace from the center point one-half the total number of spaces —in this case, half of 40, or 20.  Set the left margin stop here.
7. Tap the space bar 16 times for the longest item in the first column plus 6 more for the spaces between the columns, a total of 22 spaces. Set your **tab stop** at this point for the second column.
8. Type the two columns across the paper, using the tabular bar or key to jump the carriage to the second column.

5. **Self-Testing Work:** (30 Minutes)  See whether you can center vertically and horizontally the following 3 tabulations.  Arrange each on a separate sheet.

**Problem 1.** (Center on a full sheet of paper)

PRINCIPAL AMERICAN CITIES

| | |
|---|---|
| New York | Pittsburgh |
| Chicago | Milwaukee |
| Philadelphia | Houston |
| | |
| Los Angeles | Buffalo |
| Detroit | New Orleans |
| Baltimore | Minneapolis |
| | |
| Cleveland | Cincinnati |
| St. Louis | Seattle |
| Washington, D. C. | Kansas City |
| | |
| Boston | Newark |
| San Francisco | Dallas |

**Problem 2.** (Center on a half sheet of paper)

NOTE: A half sheet of standard typing paper accommodates 33 lines from top to bottom.

TEN LARGEST STATES

| Texas | Nevada |
|---|---|
| California | Colorado |
| Montana | Wyoming |
| New Mexico | Oregon |
| Arizona | Utah |

**Problem 3.** (Center on a half sheet of paper)

PRINCIPAL RIVERS

| Nile | Mackenzie |
|---|---|
| Amazon | Mekong |
| Mississippi-Missouri | Amur |
| | |
| Yangtze | Hwang Ho |
| Lena | Niger |
| Congo | Yenisey |

**6. Symbol Review:** (5 Minutes) The following 9 lines stress:

" (Quotation Marks)

\# (Number Sign)

' (Apostrophe)

Aim for a perfect copy.

*If keys lock, press margin release.*

```
f$f j&j f%f j_j d#d k'k s"s d#d s"s d#d k'k s"s k'k
Boys' shoes; Men's shirts; Girls' dresses; Ladies' hose;
Men's boots; Boys' slacks; Girls' jackets; Ladies' hose;

d#d k'k s"s d#d k'k s"s d#d k'k d#d s"s k'k d#d s"s
#2 pen; #7 pump; #6 jack; #8 catalog; #60 price list;
#3 ink; #9 jack; #4 pump; #9 catalog; #20 price list;

d#d s"s k'k d#d s"s k'k d#d s"s k'k d#d s"s k'k d#d
Ben's car, a "Ford," is parked in front of Joe's home.
Jim's car, a "Nash," is parked in front of Ken's home.
```

# LESSON 34

**Aim:** (a) To develop sustained typing skill by 5-Minute Timings.
(b) To learn 3-Column Tabulation.

## 1. Machine Adjustments:
    (a) Paper Guide: At 0.
    (b) Line Space Gauge: For Single Spacing.
    (c) Margin Stops: For **Pica** type................................at 15 and 70.
                    For **Elite** type.........................at 25 and 80.
    (d) Top Margin: 10 lines from top edge of paper.

## 2. Warmup:
(5 Minutes) Copy the first two lines exactly as shown; then throw the carriage twice and type the sentence 10 times:

```
frf juj ded kik sws lol aqa ;p; fvf jmj fbf jnj fgf jhj
dcd k,k sxs l.l aza ;/; ;¢; ;½; ;-; ;¢; ;½; ;-; frf juj
```

```
The puzzled judge was vexed at the quarrelsome witness.
```

## 3. Skill-Building Work:
(20 minutes)
    (a) Preview Practice on Words and Phrases................ 3 minutes
    (b) Two 1-Minute Timings and Word Practice............... 3 minutes
    (c) Two 5-Minute Timings and Word Practice...............14 minutes
                                                <u>20 minutes</u>

**First:** **Preview Practice.** Each word and phrase 3 times:

```
success...quality...holding...letting...ability
shifted...between...failures...ordinary...dislodge
pluggers...stickers...knuckling...you can...to that
on the...you will...and the
```

**Second: Machine Adjustments for Timed Typing.**
    (a) Clear all tab stops.
    (b) Set a tab stop 5 spaces from left margin.
    (c) Set line space gauge for **double** spacing.

**Third: Two 1-Minute Timings.**

```
                         5
      You can make your life a success if you take hold
10                           15                          20
and never let go.  Most men and women owe their success
              25        27
to that quality of holding on.
```

164

**Fourth: Two 5-Minute Timings.**

```
                               5
        You can make your life a success if you take hold
10                          15                          20
and never let go.  Most men and women owe their success
                    25                          30
to that quality of holding on; while most, if not all,
             35
failures result from letting go.
                40                          45
        Success comes from knuckling down to hard work
                50                          55
and being on the job every day.  The best jobs are
                60                          65
held by ordinary people--who won't let go.
                        70
        You will find failures in the ranks of men and
75                          80
women of more than ordinary ability.  They shifted
85                          90                          95
jobs so often that they could not get hold on any job.
                        100                         105
By the time they were ready to settle down, they found
                    110                         115         117
they could not dislodge the pluggers and the stickers.
```

4. **New Work Tryout:** (15 Minutes) 3-Column Tabulation.
Planning and typing a 3-column tabulation is almost the same as planning and typing a 2-column tabulation. The only difference is that you set two tab stops (one for the second column, one for the third column). As before, leave 6 blank spaces between columns. Let us work out, step by step, the following tabulation:

NEW YORK'S TALLEST BUILDINGS

| | | |
|---|---|---|
| Empire State | Metropolitan Life | Singer |
| Chrysler | Chanin | U. S. Court House |
| 60 Wall Tower | Lincoln | Municipal |
| | | |
| Chase Manhattan Bank | Irving Trust | Continental Bank |
| R. C. A. | General Electric | Sherry-Netherland |
| Woolworth | Waldorf-Astoria | Socony-Mobil |
| | | |
| City Bank | 10 East 40th Street | New York Central |
| 500 Fifth Avenue | New York Life | Transportation |

First:    **Machine Adjustments.**
         (a) Move margin stops to opposite ends.
         (b) Clear all tab stops.
         (c) Set line space gauge for single spacing.

Second:  Insert paper, top edge even with alignment scale.

Third:    Determine **vertical placement**—for equal top and bottom margins. Follow these steps:
1. Count the typewritten lines. (9)
2. Count the blank lines between the typewritten lines. (3)
3. Add: 9 plus 3 is 12. The tabulation occupies 12 lines.
4. Subtract 12 lines from 66—the total number of lines on a full sheet of standard typing paper. 12 from 66 is 54. The 54 remaining blank lines are divided in half—for equal top and bottom margins.
5. Divide 54 by 2. Result: 27.
6. Space 27 times from top edge of paper.
7. Move the carriage to the center of the paper—42 (Pica); 50 (Elite).
8. Center and type the heading—NEW YORK'S TALLEST BUILDINGS. Then space down twice for the next step—horizontal placement.

Fourth:  Determine **horizontal placement** for equal left and right margins. Follow these steps:
1. For each column in the tabulation, draw a horizontal line:

———————————————    ———————————————    ———————————————

2. Write on the lines the number of letters and spaces in the longest item in each column:

    20                  19                  17

3. Between the lines, write the number of spaces to leave between the columns. As before, leave 6 spaces:

    20      6      19      6      17

4. Add the figures in step 3:

$$20 + 6 + 19 + 6 + 17 = 68$$

The tabulation is 68 horizontal spaces.
5. Move the carriage to the center of the paper: 42 (Pica); 50 (Elite).
6. Backspace from the center point one-half the total number of spaces —in this case, half of 68, or 34; and set the left margin stop here.
7. Tap the space bar 20 times—for the longest item in the first column

plus 6 more for the spaces between the first and second columns, a total of 26 spaces.  Set a **tab stop** at this point for the second column.

8. Tap the space bar 19 times—for the longest item in the second column plus 6 more for the spaces between the second and third columns, a total of 25 spaces.  Set a **tab stop** at this point for the third column.

9. Type the three columns across the paper, using the tabular bar or key to jump the carriage from column to column as each line is typed.

5. Self-Testing Work:  (30 Minutes)  See how well you can center the following 3 tabulations.  Arrange each on a separate sheet.

**Problem 1.**  (Center on a full sheet of paper)

WORLD'S LARGEST COUNTRIES

| | | |
|---|---|---|
| Russia | Argentina | Iran |
| Canada | Sudan | Mongolia |
| China | Fr. Equatorial Africa | Saudi Arabia |
| | | |
| Brazil | Belgian Congo | Indonesia |
| United States | Algeria | Alaska |
| Australia | Greenland | Peru |
| | | |
| Fr. West Africa | Mexico | Angola |
| India | Libya | Union of So. Africa |

**Problem 2.**  (Center on a half sheet of paper)

REMINDER:  A half sheet of standard typing paper accommodates 33 lines from top to bottom.

EXPRESSIONS WRITTEN AS ONE WORD

| | | |
|---|---|---|
| today | without | classroom |
| tonight | inasmuch | beforehand |
| tomorrow | somewhat | standpoint |
| together | within | likewise |
| herein | everybody | railroad |
| hardware | meanwhile | postmaster |
| tryout | something | herewith |

**Problem 3.** (Center on a half sheet of paper)

### WORDS FREQUENTLY MISSPELLED

| | | |
|---|---|---|
| absence | chargeable | maintenance |
| absolutely | convenient | noticeable |
| accessible | correspondent | occurred |
| accidentally | counterfeit | pageant |
| accrued | customary | pamphlet |
| acquaintance | dependent | procedure |
| allotted | discipline | questionnaire |
| apparently | distinguished | recommend |
| assistance | eligible | religious |
| associate | embarrass | restaurant |

6. **Symbol Review:** (5 Minutes) The following 12 lines stress:

> ( ) (Parentheses)
> ? (Question Mark)
> : (Colon)

Copy them exactly as shown.

```
1(1 ;); ;?; ;:; 1(1 ;); ;?; ;:; 1(1 ;); ;?; ;:;
The lease read:  Rental to be Forty Dollars ($40).
The lease read:  Rental to be Sixty Dollars ($60).

How much?  How soon?  How many?  How good?  How often?
Where is Maxim?  Do you think he is in the auditorium?
Where is Frank?  Do you think he is in the laboratory?

1(1 ;); ;?; ;:; 1(1 ;); ;?; ;:; 1(1 ;); ;?; ;:;
Dr. Zinman will be in his office today at 10:15 a.m.
Dr. Saxton will be in his office today at 12:30 p.m.

The price of "America" (1953 edition) now is $2.50.
The price of "Victory" (1948 edition) now is $1.75.
The price of "Germany" (1952 edition) now is $3.50.
```

# LESSON 35

**Aim:** (a) To develop sustained typing skill by 5-Minute Timings.

(b) To learn 3-Column Tabulation with Column Headings.

## 1. Machine Adjustments:

(a) Paper Guide: At 0.

(b) Line Space Gauge: For Single Spacing.

(c) Margin Stops: For Pica type......................at 15 and 70.

For Elite type........................at 25 and 80.

(d) Top Margin: 10 lines from top edge of paper.

## 2. Warmup: (5 Minutes) Copy the first two lines exactly as shown; then throw the carriage twice and type the sentence 10 times:

```
frf juj ftf jyj fgf jhj fbf jnj fvf jmj ded kik sws lol
aqa ;p; dcd k,k sxs l.l aqa ;/; aqa ;p; aza ;/; sxs l.l
```

Six or seven flashing new jet planes quickly zoomed by.

## 3. Skill-Building Work: (20 Minutes)

(a) Preview Practice on Words and Phrases.................. 3 minutes

(b) Two 1-Minute Timings and Word Practice............... 3 minutes

(c) Two 5-Minute Timings and Word Practice...............14 minutes

20 minutes

First:   **Preview Practice.** Each word and phrase 3 times:

```
worked...quit...trying...better...amount...future
always...change...decided...another...building...
finished...realized...interested...accomplished...
at the...he had...to do...did not...it is
```

Second: **Machine Adjustments for Timed Typing.**

(a) Clear all tab stops.

(b) Set a tab stop 5 spaces from left margin.

(c) Set line space gauge for **double** spacing.

Third:   **Two 1-Minute Timings.**

```
                     5
     When Henry Ford was making his first car in a
        10                        15
small brick building at the rear of his home, he
        20                   23
worked day and night.
```

169

Fourth:  Two 5-Minute Timings.

```
                                    5
        When Henry Ford was making his first car in a
        10                        15
small brick building at the rear of his home, he
        20                        25
worked day and night.  He was very much interested
        30                        35
in what he was trying to create.  When he had finished
        40                        45                        50
it, his interest waned.  He felt he had accomplished
                          55
what he had set out to do.
                          60
        But he began to think.  He realized that if he
        65                        70                        75
quit now, and did not try to build a better car than
                          80                        85
his first one, his life would not amount to much.  So
                    90                        95
he decided to start right away to make a better car.
                    100                       105
He saw a future for his car, and so he went to work
                    110                       115
again with all his might, and made a car better than

his first.
                    120                       125
        It is always too soon to quit.  Change your plans,
        130                       135           138
if you must, take another hold, but never quit.
```

4. **New Work Tryout:** (15 Minutes) 3-Column Tabulation with Column Headings. Planning and typing a 3-column tabulation with column headings is almost the same as planning and typing a 3-column tabulation without column headings. The only difference is that you center the column headings over the columns. Let us work out, step by step, the following tabulation:

## FAMOUS WORLD EXPOSITIONS

| Exposition | Year | Place |
|---|---|---|
| Louisiana Purchase | 1904 | St. Louis |
| Panama-Pacific | 1915 | San Francisco |
| Sesquicentennial | 1926 | Philadelphia |
| Century of Progress | 1933 | Chicago |
| Texas Centennial | 1936 | Dallas |
| New York World's Fair | 1939 | New York |

**First:** **Machine Adjustments.**
(a) Move margin stops to opposite ends.
(b) Clear all tab stops.
(c) Set line space gauge for single spacing.

**Second:** Insert paper, top edge even with alignment scale.

**Third:** Determine **vertical placement**—for equal top and bottom margins. Follow these steps:
1. Count the typewritten lines. (8)
2. Count the blank lines between the typewritten lines. (4)
3. ADD: 8 plus 4 is 12. The tabulation occupies 12 lines.
4. Subtract 12 lines from 66—the total number of lines on a full sheet of standard typing paper. 12 from 66 is 54. The 54 remaining blank lines are divided in half—for equal top and bottom margins.
5. Divide 54 by 2. Result: 27.
6. Space 27 times from top edge of paper.
7. Move the carriage to the center of the paper: 42 (Pica); 50 (Elite).
8. Center and type the main heading—FAMOUS WORLD EXPOSITIONS. Then space down 4 times for the next step—horizontal placement.

> NOTE: You will center the column headings after you have typed the body of the tabulation.

**Fourth:** Determine **horizontal placement**—for equal left and right margins.
1. For each column in the tabulation, draw a horizontal line.

_____         _____         _____

2. Write on the lines the number of letters and spaces in the longest item in each column:

    21                 4                 13
_____         _____         _____

3. Between the lines, write the number of spaces to leave between the columns. As before, leave 6 spaces:

| 21 | 6 | 4 | 6 | 13 |
|----|---|---|---|----|

4. Add the figures in Step 3:

$$21 + 6 + 4 + 6 + 13 = 50$$

5. Move the carriage to the center of the paper—42 (Pica); 50 (Elite).
6. Backspace from the center point one-half the total number of spaces —in this case, half of 50, or 25; and set the left margin stop here.
7. Tap the space bar 21 times—for the longest item in the first column plus 6 more for the spaces between the first and second columns— a total of 27 spaces. Set a **tab stop** at this point for the second column.
8. Tap the space bar 4 times—for the longest item in the second column plus 6 more for the spaces between the second and third columns—a total of 10 spaces. Set your **tab stop** at this point for the third column.
9. Now type the 3 columns across the paper—using the tabulator bar or key—to jump the carriage from column to column as each line is typed.
10. Center the column headings—as follows:
    (a) Roll the paper back to the main heading.
    (b) Space down twice from the main heading—for the column headings.
    (c) Move the carriage to the center of the first column. Backspace **once** for every two letters in *Exposition*. Then type the word and underscore it.

*The center of a column is half the number of spaces in the longest item.*

    (d) Jump the carriage to the first **tab stop**. Type the word *Year* and underscore it.
    (e) Move the carriage to the center of the third column. Backspace **once** for every two letters in *Place*. Then type the word and underscore it.

5. **Self-Testing Work:** (30 Minutes) Here are two more 3-column tabulations with column headings. Arrange each on a full sheet of paper.

## Problem 1.

### HISTORICAL AMERICAN DOCUMENTS

| Description | Author | Date |
|---|---|---|
| Letter | Christopher Columbus | 1493 |
| Epitaph | Benjamin Franklin | 1776 |
| Common Sense | Thomas Paine | 1776 |
| Bill for Religious Freedom | Thomas Jefferson | 1784 |
| The Star-Spangled Banner | Francis Scott Key | 1814 |
| The Gettysburg Address | Abraham Lincoln | 1863 |

## Problem 2.

### BASEBALL CLUBS

| City | Team | League |
|---|---|---|
| Baltimore | Orioles | American |
| Boston | Red Sox | American |
| Brooklyn | Dodgers | National |
| Chicago | Cubs | National |
| Chicago | White Sox | American |
| Cincinnati | Red Legs | National |
| Cleveland | Indians | American |
| Detroit | Tigers | American |
| Kansas City | Athletics | American |
| Milwaukee | Braves | National |
| New York | Yankees | American |
| New York | Giants | National |
| Philadelphia | Phillies | National |
| Pittsburgh | Pirates | National |
| St. Louis | Cardinals | National |
| Washington | Senators | American |

**6. Symbol Review:** (5 Minutes) The following 12 lines stress:

         @ (at)

         ¼ (one-quarter)

         * (asterisk)

Copy them exactly as shown:

```
;@; ;¼; ;*; ;@; ;¼; ;*; ;@; ;¼; ;*; ;@; ;¼; ;*;
The invoice read:  75 pairs @ 45¼¢; 5% discount.
The invoice read:  80 pairs @ 58¼¢; 3% discount.

;@; ;¼; ;*; ;@; ;¼; ;*; ;@; ;¼; ;*; ;@; ;¼; ;*;
The bank increased the interest rate from 2¼% to 3¼%.
The bank increased the interest rate from 3¼% to 4¼%.

;@; ;¼; ;*; ;@; ;¼; ;*; ;@; ;¼; ;*; ;@; ;¼; ;*;
The symbols ¢ @ and % are often used in statements.
The symbols % @ and ¢ are often used in statements.

;@; ;¼; ;*; ;@; ;¼; ;*; ;@; ;¼; ;*; ;@; ;¼; ;*;
The * (asterisk) is frequently used for footnotes.
The * (asterisk) is frequently used for footnotes.
```

# SUPPLEMENTS

## 1.

## COMMON ERRORS AND HOW TO OVERCOME THEM

Here are some of the errors you may make until your typing skill is fully developed. You can easily avoid these errors by studying the cause and improving the technique suggested for remedying them:

| TYPE OF ERROR | PROBABLE CAUSE | SUGGESTED REMEDY |
|---|---|---|
| 1. Omission of space. | Typing too fast. | Slow down a bit. Type with better control of your fingers. |
| 2. Too many spaces. | Pushing the spacebar. | Strike the spacebar sharply—as though it were red hot. |
| 3. Shadowed letters. | Pushing the keys. | Strike each key with the fingertip —sharply. Release instantly. |
| 4. Omitted letters. | Typing too fast. | Slow down a bit. Type with better control of your fingers. Spell the words as you type. |
| 5. Raised capital letters. | Releasing the shift key too soon. | Hold the shift key until you have struck the letter key. |
| 6. Omitted or inserted words. | Losing your place in the copy. | Keep your eyes on the copy—even when throwing the carriage for a new line. |
| 7. Uneven left margin. | Throwing the carriage too slowly or too sharply. | Practice throwing the carriage with the same force after each line. |

## 2.

## PUNCTUATION SPACING

| RULE | *Example* |
|---|---|
| 1. Space Once— | |
| (a) After a comma. | We need eggs, butter, and milk. |
| (b) After a semicolon. | Taste it; you may like it. |
| (c) After the period in an abbreviation. | Mr. and Mrs. Weston have arrived. |

| RULE | *Example* |
|---|---|
| (d) Between a whole number and a "made" fraction. | The pencil is 5 1/2 inches long. (BUT:  The pencil is 5½ inches long) |
| (e) Before and after the ampersand. | Mary is a cashier at the May & Co. store. |
| (f) After the exclamation mark **within** a sentence. | What! you haven't finished it yet? |

## 2. Space Twice—

| | |
|---|---|
| (a) After the period at the end of a sentence. | John Paul Jones was born in Scotland.  He is known as the "Father of the American Navy." |
| (b) After a colon. | The teacher said:  "Strike the keys with the fingertips." |

## 3. Do Not Space—

| | |
|---|---|
| (a) Between parentheses and the words they enclose. | Mr. Van Dusen (bookkeeper) opened the safe. |
| (b) Between quotation marks and the words they enclose. | Franklin D. Roosevelt said: "The one thing we have to fear is fear itself." |
| (c) Before or after the hyphen in compound words. | His brother-in-law is in the Navy. |
| (d) Before or after the dash. | Every champion was once a beginner--with ambition. |
| (e) Before or after a decimal point. | The bonds yield 3.5% interest. |
| (f) Before or after a comma in numerals. | The sun is 1,305,000 times as large as the earth. |
| (g) Between the # symbol and numerals. | Invoice #890 amounts to $305.60. |
| (h) Before or after the apostrophe. | Joe's car is in the garage. |
| (i) Before the % symbol. | Savings Banks pay 3¼% interest. |
| (j) Before the symbols used for feet and inches. | The room is 8' 3" long. |
| (k) Before or after the colon in time of day. | Our train leaves at 1:30 p.m. |

### 3.
## RULES FOR DIVIDING WORDS AT THE END OF A LINE

1. Divide a word only between syllables.
   EXAMPLES: con-tain, pro-gram, trans-act.

2. Divide a word between consonants.
   EXAMPLES: let-ter, rub-ber, begin-ning.

   **But:** If a word is derived from a word ending in a double consonant, divide after the second consonant:
   EXAMPLES: tall-est, add-ing.

3. Divide a word after the prefix.
   EXAMPLES: be-tween, sub-mit, dis-appoint.

4. Divide a word before the suffix.
   EXAMPLES: lov-ing, judg-ment.

5. Divide a hyphenated word only on the hyphen.
   EXAMPLES: self-confidence, attorney-general.
   NOTE: All words beginning with *self* are hyphenated, except **selfish**.

6. Do not divide a word of one syllable.
   EXAMPLES: please, height, through.

7. Do not carry over ed, er, ly. Finish the word.
   EXAMPLES: tested, rather, lovely.

8. Do not divide proper names.
   EXAMPLES: George, Friday, Buffalo.

9. Do not separate the title from the name.
   EXAMPLES: Mr. Hudson, Dr. Miller.

10. Do not divide figures, contractions, or abbreviations.
    EXAMPLES: $2,500,000; C. O. D.; wasn't; 7:30 p.m.

11. Do not divide four letter words.
    EXAMPLES: only, rely, upon.

12. Do not divide the last word on a page.

13. Do not divide the last word in a paragraph.
    NOTE: When in doubt, find out. **Consult the Dictionary.**

## 4.

## FACILITY SENTENCE PRACTICE

Repeated practice of the following sentences will boost your typing speed. Type each sentence 10 times.

Margin Stops:  For **Pica** Type............15 and 70
For **Elite** Type............25 and 80

|    |                                                        | 5-Stroke Words |
|----|--------------------------------------------------------|:--------------:|
| 1. | Mix work with pluck--for luck.                         | 6  |
| 2. | Every champion was once a beginner.                    | 7  |
| 3. | The empty can makes the most noise.                    | 7  |
| 4. | Try to be thorough in everything you do.               | 8  |
| 5. | Money is most useful when it circulates.               | 8  |
| 6. | An expert is one who excels in his work.               | 8  |
| 7. | If you look for trouble, you will find fault.          | 9  |
| 8. | A good way to win an argument is to avoid it.          | 9  |
| 9. | To win friends, show yourself to be friendly.          | 9  |
| 10.| Be a live wire; then no one will step on you.          | 9  |
| 11.| The dumb person is one who is always talking.          | 9  |
| 12.| You must pay the price to excel in your work.          | 9  |
| 13.| Talk may be cheap but not over the telephone.          | 9  |
| 14.| To make good, you must have the will to make good.     | 10 |
| 15.| A grudge is too heavy a load for any man to carry.     | 10 |
| 16.| The world pays very well to those who really know.     | 10 |
| 17.| Never try to get even; better strive to get ahead.     | 10 |
| 18.| Help your fellow workers if you want to be helped.     | 10 |
| 19.| You cannot see the future, but it is always before you.| 11 |
| 20.| Your mind is like a parachute; it works only when open.| 11 |

```
        1    2    3    4    5    6    7    8    9    10   11
```

5.

## ALPHABETIC SENTENCE PRACTICE

Alphabetic sentences are very useful for review and for obtaining a thorough command of the keyboard. Each of the following sentences contains every letter of the alphabet. Repeated thoughtful typing of these sentences will help you master the keyboard and make you a skillful typist.

### DIRECTIONS

1. **Machine Adjustments.**
   (a) Clear all tab stops.
   (b) Set margin stops: For **Pica Type**. . . . . . . . . . . . . . . . . . . . . . . . . . .at 15 and 70.
                       For **Elite Type**. . . . . . . . . . . . . . . . . . . .at 25 and 80.
   (c) Set a tab stop 5 spaces from your left margin.
   (d) Set line space gauge for **single** spacing.

2. **Practice Procedure.**
   (a) Type the first sentence 5 times.
   (b) Check your work. Make a list of the words in which you find errors.
   (c) Practice each word until you can type it smoothly and accurately.
   (d) Type the sentence again 5 times. Aim for greater accuracy.
      NOTE: (a) Try two sentences each day.
               (b) When you have tried them all, repeat this procedure.

                   5

1.      Joseph Boxer packed my sledge with five dozen
       10
   quails.

                 5                             10

2.      Peter Fahb quickly mixed two dozen jugs of liquid
       11
   veneer.

                 5

3.      The job requires extra pluck and zeal from every
     10              13
   young wage earner.

                 5

4.      The jovial chemist quickly analyzed the mixture
     10              14
   of brown and green powder.

                 5

5.      The queer, lazy witness from Kansas vexed the
     10              14
   capable, patient old judge.

                                    5                                        10

6.       John Wilborg, trapeze artist, executed his famous
                    15
jumping act very quickly.
                          5

7.       Joe Quick, brainy government expert, was amazed
         10                  15           18
to find numerous errors in the tax report.
                          5

8.       You can make good on your job and even excel in
         10                  15           19
your work if you perform every task with quiet zeal.
                          5

9.       Our laboratory has just developed an amazing new
         10                  15                  20
wax that quickly restores the original finish on all
                    22
furniture.
                          5

10.      John Quinn improved his typewriting skill by
         10                  15
seizing every opportunity to practice effective speed-
      20                  23
building exercises.

## 6.

## ACCURACY AND SPEED PRACTICE

    Accuracy and speed will come to you with thoughtful repetition practice. Devote a definite amount of time for practice each day. To reach your highest speed and accuracy, keep constantly in mind the following points:

1. Strike each key only with the finger that controls it. Strike the keys squarely in the center with the fingertip—quickly and sharply.
2. Keep your fingers curved like claws—close to the home keys.
3. Move your fingers only. Keep your arms and elbows close to your sides.
4. Type by touch only. Keep your eyes on the copy—even when throwing the carriage for a new line.
5. Type the common words as a unit, not letter by letter. For example, when typing the word the, don't spell it to yourself (t-h-e). Think of it and type it as a unit (the). Form this habit, and you will soon be a faster and more accurate typist.

## 7.

## HOW TO DETERMINE YOUR SPEED
### (In Correct Words Per Minute)

To determine your typing speed in Correct Words Per Minute, on a 5-minute timing:

1. Note the number *nearest* the last word you typed. That number represents the total words you typed.
2. Subtract 1 for each error from the total words typed.
3. Divide the remainder by 5—because you typed for 5 minutes.

EXAMPLE: Assume that in the first 5-minute test in supplement 8, you typed through the word *name* in the last paragraph and made 4 errors.

The number nearest the word *name* is 105. This means that you typed 105 words in 5 minutes. So to determine your typing speed in Correct Words Per Minute, jot down:

Total Words Typed .............................. 105
Subtract (4 Errors x 1) ........................... –4
Correct Words Typed ...........................5/101
Correct Words Per Minute........ .............. 20⅕

Your typing speed in Correct Words Per Minute was 20 words.

Fractions less than ½ are dropped.
Fractions ½ and over count as whole numbers.

## 8.

## HOW TO USE THE 5-MINUTE TIMED TESTS
### (Pages 182, 183, 184, 185)

1. Use them for practice and for timing yourself. Aim for **speed** and **accuracy.**
2. Set margin stops at 15 and 70 (Pica); 25 and 80 (Elite).
Set a Tab Stop 5 spaces from your left margin.
Set line space gauge for **double** spacing.
3. Type each paragraph in a selected test two times; then time yourself for 5 minutes on the entire copy. When you have tried every test, start over again from the beginning.
4. Check your work. Make a list of the words in which you find errors. Practice each word until you can type it smoothly and accurately.
5. If you have difficulty with certain letters, practice the appropriate Corrective Drill in Supplement 9.

REMINDER: (1) Take two 5-minute tests on the same copy.
(2) Determine your typing speed in Correct Words Per Minute on each test.
(3) Enter the better of the two scores in your Personal Progress Record which you started in Lesson 15.

## CIVIL-SERVICE TYPING TESTS

5
    Our Federal, State, and City Governments employ
10                              15
an army of typists.  To fill the constant need for
20                              25
such workers, tests are held at frequent intervals.
    30                              35
        To take a Federal, State, or City civil-service
    40                                  45
test, you first file an application with the appro-
    50                                  55                                  60
priate Civil Service Commission.  If your application
                        65                              70
is approved, you are sent a notice of when and where
                    75
to report for the test.
                                        80
        Each Civil Service Commission--Federal, State,
    85                          90                                  95
City--maintains a register of the candidates available
                            100                              105
for appointment.  The place which your name occupies
                        110                              115
on the register is determined by your grade in the
                        120                              125
test.  The higher your grade, the better chance you
                        130
have for securing a job.

*Repeat if you finish before end of 5 minutes.*

## MEANING OF CREDIT

5
Credit is the power of obtaining something today
10                              15                              20
in return for future payment.  When you buy supplies
25                              30
at the grocery to be paid for on the first of the
35
following month, credit is used.
40                              45
Credit is confidence that the borrower will repay.
50                              55
This confidence rests upon the character of the borrower
60                              65
and his ability and willingness to pay at a definite

time.
70                              75
About 10 per cent of business is carried on by
80                              85
cash; about 90 per cent is carried on by credit through
90                              95
the use of credit instruments.
100                             105
Checks, notes, bonds, are a few examples of credit
110                             115
instruments.  They serve as substitutes for money and
120                             125
do away with the need for a vast amount of actual money
130                             135
which would be required without their use.

*Repeat if you finish before end of 5 minutes.*

## TODInY IS HERE

TODAY IS HERE

                              5
        Today is here.  Do not waste time; the time you
    10                          15                          20
wasted yesterday is lost forever.  Do not worry about
                      25
what may happen.  Do the things you should do.
        30                          35
        Today is here.  Do not look back at the past.
        40                          45
Look forward.  Do not imagine what you would do if
        50                          55
things were different.  You can make good with the
        60
assets you have.
                              65                          70
        Today is here.  Be kind to people; avoid hurting
                      75                          80
them.  Look for good qualities, not faults.  People,
              85
not things, are most important.
                  90                          95
        Today is here.  Study to improve yourself, for
            100                         105
you should be prepared.  It is the surest way to

succeed.
            110                         115
        Today is here.  Make the most of it.  Do not
            120                         125
wait for tomorrow.  Tomorrow never comes.

                        *Repeat if you finish before end of 5 minutes.*

## LETTER WRITING

        5
     Every business letter you receive gives you an
   10                        15
impression of two people--the person who signed it
   20                        25
and the person who typed it.  This applies to the
      30
letters you type.
                  35                        40
     You may not be responsible for the way the
                     45                        50
letter is composed--the way in which the dictator
                     55                        60
has expressed his thoughts; but you are responsible
                  65
for its typewritten appearance.
                     70                        75
     Make your letters look attractive.  You can do
                  80                        85
so by accurate typing, artistic placement, correct
                  90                        95
grammar, spelling, and punctuation.  If something in
                  100                       105
the letter does not seem to make sense, ask the dic-

tator about it.
      110                       115
     Every office requires its letters to be typed
   120                        125
according to certain standard letter forms.  The
      130                       135
three most popular forms are known as block,
            140                       145
indented, and semiblock.  Models of these forms
               150
are in this book.

               *Repeat if you finish before end of 5 minutes.*

## 9.

## CORRECTIVE DRILLS

| | | | | | | | |
|---|---|---|---|---|---|---|---|
| a<br>drill | aboard | absent | absorb | accept | actual | action | advice |
| b<br>drill | bought | belong | behave | before | beauty | battle | basket |
| c<br>drill | carpet | charge | common | copies | coming | church | change |
| d<br>drill | design | detail | devote | direct | depend | depart | dances |
| e<br>drill | effort | employ | enjoys | entire | escape | effect | either |
| f<br>drill | future | friend | Friday | forget | follow | finish | filled |
| g<br>drill | ground | glance | giving | garage | garter | gather | gently |
| h<br>drill | handle | happen | height | honest | houses | hungry | hotels |
| i<br>drill | import | indeed | impose | inborn | income | Indian | indent |
| j<br>drill | jacket | jungle | juggle | jumble | joined | jovial | judges |
| k<br>drill | kettle | kidnap | kindly | knight | knives | knotty | knaves |
| l<br>drill | larger | lately | lawful | labors | ledger | letter | liable |
| m<br>drill | member | mental | method | middle | mighty | mailed | manner |
| n<br>drill | notice | ninety | number | nerves | native | narrow | neatly |
| o<br>drill | object | oblige | offers | orange | origin | outlet | overdo |
| p<br>drill | pencil | parcel | parade | parent | papers | pamper | patent |
| q<br>drill | quaint | Quaker | quarts | quench | quotes | quoted | quotas |
| r<br>drill | reduce | razors | reader | reason | record | region | remote |
| s<br>drill | search | second | scheme | sample | salute | silver | saucer |

```
t
drill       tender theory tavern temper thread thrift throng
u
drill       umpire uncles unique unlike untold unpack unload
v
drill       vanity valise vacant valley vanish virtue visits
w
drill       weight waited warmed wasted weapon weaver wheels
x
drill       excuse excite excess except exceed exhale exists
y
drill       yachts yellow yields yearly yonder yelled yawned
z
drill       zenith zipper zigzag zephyr zebras zealot zoning
```

## 10.

### ERASING

Erasing wastes time. You can type 20 words in the time required to make one neat erasure, and many more if carbon copies are involved. So strive for accuracy. However, even the expert typist occasionally makes an error; so you should know how to make erasures neatly.

**To Make a Neat Erasure:**

1. Be sure your hands and eraser are clean. Clean the eraser by rubbing it briskly on white paper, or on fine-grained sandpaper.
2. Move the carriage to the left or right to prevent erasure grit from falling into the machine.
3. Roll the paper up until the error to be erased is on top of the roller. Hold the paper firmly by pressing it against the roller with your finger tips.
4. Erase the error with a light, short, circular motion, blowing lightly to keep the grit out of the machine.
5. Return the paper to the typing position and strike the correct letter lightly; then backspace and strike it again until the letter is as dark as the other letters on the sheet.

   NOTE: 1. Use a typewriter eraser on the original copy; a soft pencil eraser on carbon copies.
   2. Protect carbon copies from smudging by placing a small piece of paper under each carbon paper.
   3. Erase on the original copy first; then remove one piece of protective paper at a time and erase the carbon copies.

## 11.

## ADDRESSING ENVELOPES

The most widely used business envelopes are:

1. The commercial or No. 6 envelope (6½ inches by 3⅝ inches).
2. The legal or No. 10 envelope (9½ inches by 4⅛ inches).

**To Address a No. 6 Envelope:**
1. Insert envelope, flap edge first, left edge at 0 on scale.
2. Space 12 single lines from top edge of envelope.
3. Move carriage to 25 on scale (Pica); 35 (Elite).
4. Type address in block form.

**To Address a No. 10 Envelope:**
1. Insert envelope, flap edge first, left edge at 0 on scale.
2. Space 14 single lines from top edge of envelope.
3. Move carriage to 40 on scale (Pica); 50 (Elite).
4. Type address in block form.

> NOTE: 1. Use double spacing for a 3-line address.
> 2. Use single spacing for an address of 4 lines or more.
> 3. Type annotations such as *Attention. Hold. Personal.*, 3 single lines below the address and 3 spaces from 0 on the scale.

## 12.

## FOLDING LETTERS

### For No. 6 Envelope
(6½ inches by 3⅝ inches)

1. Fold from the bottom to within about ⅛ inch of the top edge. (See Fig. 18)

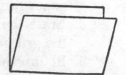

Fig. 18.

2. Fold from right to left a little less than ⅓ of the width. (See Fig. 19)

Fig. 19.

3. Fold again from left to right, leaving about ⅛ inch margin. (See Fig. 20)

Fig. 20.

4. Insert the folded letter in the envelope.
   (a) Hold the envelope with the reverse side facing you.
   (b) Insert folded letter with margin at top. (See Fig. 21)

Fig. 21.

### For No. 10 Envelope
(9½ inches by 4⅛ inches)

1. Fold from the bottom to a little less than ⅓ of the sheet. (See Fig. 22)

Fig. 22.

2. Fold again to within about ⅛ of an inch from the top edge. (See Fig. 23)

Fig. 23.

3. Insert the folded letter into the envelope.
   (a) Hold the envelope with the reverse side facing you.
   (b) Insert the letter with the margin at the top. (See Fig. 24)

Fig. 24.

## 13.

## SPECIAL SYMBOLS

| SYMBOL | HOW MADE | EXAMPLE |
|---|---|---|
| Dash — | Strike the hyphen twice--without spacing.<br>Do not space before or after the dash. | Every champion was once a beginner--with ambition. |
| Exclamation Mark ! | 1. Strike the apostrophe.<br>2. Backspace.<br>3. Strike the period lightly. | Fight for your rights! |
| Multiplication Sign x | Strike the small x.<br>Space once before and after the x.<br>In measurements, the x means BY. | 5 x 10<br><br>a 9 x 15 rug. |
| Minus Sign — | Strike the hyphen.<br>Space once before and after the minus sign. | 12 - 5 |
| Division Sign ÷ | 1. Strike the hyphen.<br>2. Backspace.<br>3. Strike the colon.<br>Space once before and after the division sign. | 20 ÷ 5 |
| Plus Sign + | 1. Strike the hyphen, then backspace.<br>2. Depress the shift lock, then strike the apostrophe.<br>3. Backspace, turn the roller up slightly, then strike the apostrophe again.<br><br>Space once before and after the plus sign. | 6 + 8 |
| NOTE: | For an easy, makeshift plus sign, do this:<br>1. Strike the hyphen.<br>2. Backspace.<br>3. Strike the slant. | 6 ≠ 8 |

| SYMBOL | HOW MADE | EXAMPLE |
|---|---|---|
| Equals Sign = | 1. Strike the hyphen.<br>2. Backspace.<br>3. Turn the roller up slightly and strike the hyphen again.<br>Space once before and after the equals sign. | 5 x 10 = 50 |
| Fractions not on the keyboard | Use the slant.<br>Space once before and after the fraction. | 5 1/3<br>7/8 of an inch |
| Ditto Mark " | Use quotation mark. | March 15<br>   "   20 |
| Feet and inches (After numbers) | Use apostrophe for feet.<br>Use quotation mark for inches. | 5' 8" tall |
| Caret √ | 1. Underscore preceding letter.<br>2. Strike slant in space between words. | him<br>I saw/there. |
| Degree Sign ° | Turn the roller down slightly and strike the small o. | 85° |
| Exponents (Raised numbers) | Turn the roller down slightly and strike the desired number. | $x^2$ |
| Chemical Symbols (Lowered numbers) | Turn the roller up slightly and strike the desired number. | $H_2O$ |
| Roman Numbers | Use capital letters.<br>Sometimes small letters are used. | X L C D<br>x l c d |

## 14.

## HOW TO EXPRESS NUMBERS

*Type in Figures:*

1. Definite numbers above **ten**.
   EXAMPLE: Our office has 15 desks.

2. Round numbers in advertising.
   EXAMPLE: We distributed over 10,000 circulars.

*Type in Words:*

1. Numbers **ten** and below.
   EXAMPLE: Our house has seven rooms.

2. Round numbers, in general.
   EXAMPLE: About ten thousand people saw the game.

*Type in Figures:*

3. Numbers in a series.
   EXAMPLE: Ship 5 cartons, 8 boxes, and 10 barrels.

4. Definite ages.
   EXAMPLE: Mary is 9 years, 4 months old.

5. Numbers **ten** and above used as street names.
   EXAMPLE: The school is near 110th Street.
   He lives at 295 East 12th Street.

6. Definite amounts of money.
   EXAMPLE: Mary paid $5.00 for the hat.
   Mary paid $20 for the dress.
   NOTE: Omit the ciphers in amounts above $9.00.

7. Numbers used with percentages.
   EXAMPLE: Savings banks pay 3% interest.
   Savings banks pay 3 per cent interest.

8. Graduation and historical dates.
   EXAMPLE: The class of '42 had a reunion yesterday.
   It is thrilling to think of the spirit of '76.

9. Weights, dimensions, measurements.
   EXAMPLE: The weight is 5 pounds 4 ounces.
   The room is 12 by 15 feet.
   His height is 5 feet 7 inches.

*Type in Words:*

3. Numbers at the beginning of a sentence.
   EXAMPLE: Two hundred replies were received.

4. Ages in general.
   EXAMPLE: Mary is nine years old.

5. Numbers **ten** and below used as street names.
   EXAMPLE: Harry lives at 125 Seventh Avenue.
   NOTE: After *East, West, North, South,* type figures.
   EXAMPLE: Harry lives at 125 West 7th Street.

6. Indefinite amounts of money.
   EXAMPLE: Henry saved several hundred dollars last year.

7. Numbers used as ordinals.
   EXAMPLE: It is his twenty-third birthday.
   It is their fifth wedding anniversary.

8. Numbers used for decades and centuries.
   EXAMPLE: He told a story about the gay nineties.
   America was discovered in the fifteenth century.

9. Numbers used as proper names.
   EXAMPLE: Joe is a member of the Ninth Infantry Regiment.
   Joe lives in the Fifth Election District.